MARGARET LAURENCE

WOMEN WHO ROCK series

MARGARET LAURENCE

A Gift of Grace: A Spiritual Biography

NOELLE BOUGHTON

Women's Press
Toronto

Margaret Laurence: A Gift of Grace – A Spiritual Biography
by Noelle Boughton

First published in 2006 by
Women's Press, an imprint of Canadian Scholars' Press Inc.
180 Bloor Street West, Suite 801
Toronto, Ontario
M5S 2V6

www.womenspress.ca

Canadian Scholars' Press/Women's Press gratefully acknowledges financial support for our publishing activities from the Ontario Arts Council, the Canada Council for the Arts, the Government of Canada through the Book Publishing Industry Development Program (BPIDP), and the Government of Ontario through the Ontario Book Publishing Tax Credit Program.

Library and Archives Canada Cataloguing in Publication

Boughton, Noelle
Margaret Laurence : a gift of grace—a spiritual biography / Noelle Boughton.

Includes bibliographical references.
ISBN 0-88961-459-8

1. Laurence, Margaret, 1926–1987. 2. Laurence, Margaret, 1926–1987—Religion.
3. Novelists, Canadian (English)—20th century—Biography. I. Title.

ps8523.A862526 2006   c813'.54   c2006-904835-5

Cover design, text design and layout: Susan MacGregor/Digital Zone
Cover illustration: Muriel Romig Dawson. Reprinted by permission of the artist.

06 07 08 09 10   5 4 3 2 1

Printed and bound in Canada by Marquis Book Printing Inc.

ONTARIO ARTS COUNCIL
CONSEIL DES ARTS DE L'ONTARIO

THE CANADA COUNCIL | LE CONSEIL DES ARTS
FOR THE ARTS | DU CANADA
SINCE 1957 | DEPUIS 1957

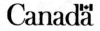

Canadä

To Ian,
for all of your support ...
and believing.

CONTENTS

CHAPTER 1

SEEKING MARGARET LAURENCE

I discovered Margaret Laurence during a Canadian literature course at the University of Manitoba in 1975. It was International Women's Year and *The Diviners* had just exploded onto the literary scene, solidifying Laurence's position as Canada's premier author. I was nineteen, a wannabe writer from small-town Manitoba who knew nothing about Laurence except that her book promised to be about a woman "toughened" by growing up in a small prairie community. I started reading with mild interest, but was soon electrified by each shock of recognition. Here were the fibres from my life—the ice-crusted mitts, nuisance grounds, and faded Jesus pictures hanging in the United Church basement. Here was Morag Gunn cracking open the constraints of relationship to reclaim her life just when many of us young women were struggling to define what that meant, let alone how to do it. Here, too, were the Métis and Scots of our prairie history. No one had laid bare our story like that before, and no writer ever rivalled her impact on me.

The Diviners hooked me and I devoured Laurence's other Manawaka books, mesmerized by her truth of place and spirit. But the more I read, the more I wondered how she created some of Canada's most powerful literature. By the time I was studying journalism in Ottawa two years later, I'd learned that she grew up in the Manitoba town next to mine and attended a United Church college in Winnipeg, but I was shocked to discover that she was also a reporter for the *Winnipeg Citizen*, the alternative 1940s daily on which I was writing my thesis. I was so intrigued by how her fiction career grew out of her journalistic foundation that I wanted to meet her, but I was too polite to ask solely to satisfy my curiosity until her former managing editor said he almost fired her for being a Communist. Then she was part of the *Citizen*'s story and I started asking to interview her, spurred on by her college roommate who had also worked for the *Citizen*.

Laurence finally agreed to an interview in 1978, and we met one beautiful fall afternoon when she was visiting her friends Walter and Margaret Swayze in Winnipeg. I don't know what I expected, but it wasn't the shy, stocky woman who looked more like a Neepawa matron in her polyester blouse, dark pants, and unfashionably cropped hair than any image I'd had of a world-famous writer. She also appeared Aboriginal, but since no one—including her—could ever trace such an ancestry, I attributed her dark eyes and high cheekbones to her Celtic heritage. Once we were talking, I also experienced a fascinating duality. On the one hand, she seemed so private, almost guarded, that I didn't feel I could trespass far beyond the bounds that we'd set for our interview. On the other, I was touched by how she answered my simple questions with such candid reflections about her life and career. There wasn't anything she wouldn't answer, but I still came away feeling that there was an underlying well I couldn't even begin to tap during that interview.

I followed the rest of Laurence's life with interest, but by the time she died in 1987, I couldn't help wondering how her later years as an anti-nuclear activist tied to her writing career. She'd had a complexity of threads that intrigued me: her work as a prairie writer, support of The Writers' Union of Canada, evidence of a spiritual call as she counted the books left to write, and impassioned activism. Her last speeches were full of references to Protestant Christianity's social gospel movement and how the next generation must face its responsibility. It was a fascinating blend, and when she died, I wanted to know more about her sense of place, social justice, community, spirituality, and the connection they had to her growing up on the prairies.

I kept looking for those answers in everything that was published on her, but each work left me disappointed. There were thick strands of what I was seeking in her posthumously published memoir, *Dance on the Earth*, but it was her story of what she wanted us to know, and didn't feel as candid as her fiction. The other essays and biographies made valiant attempts, but I finished each feeling that no one had yet excavated the essential Margaret Laurence that I sensed was there in both the woman I had met and the work that she'd published.

I grew up in the same middle-class, United Church, small-town prairie milieu as Laurence. In fact, once I started researching her life, I found little had changed in our area in the intervening decades, so I was convinced her roots had more impact on her life and work than anyone had yet acknowledged. When Canadian Scholars' Press/Women's Press asked me to reconnect with my heritage to write about her, I welcomed the opportunity to trace her sense of place, community, social justice, and spirituality to see how they began on the prairies, and influenced her life and writing.

I spent the next year studying Laurence's papers and books, and the wealth of material written about her. I combed the York, McMaster, and Trent University archives, interviewed academics and her friends and colleagues from across the country, and made pilgrimages to both of her Canadian communities—the one she was born in, Neepawa, Manitoba, and the one she died in, Lakefield, Ontario. I searched the Margaret Laurence Home's records in Neepawa—and even saw the old Remington typewriter on which she wrote most of her novels—then took a wonderful tour with a local historian and saw the Margaret Laurence and Manawaka sites in Neepawa. It was a fascinating journey, and I finally found what I was looking for. I set out trying to define the essence of Margaret Laurence's spirit, but finished having traced her spiritual journey.

Much of Laurence's truth resides in the words she left, both publicly and privately, for she was incredibly self-aware and articulate about her life's themes and where they were rooted. But her truth was scattered across the full arc of her life and tucked in her books, personal papers, and interviews. I'd never read her African books before, but I found they were the natural progression for the young woman whose sensitivities were honed on the prairies. They also formed the foundation from which the more mature writer developed her Canadian fiction.

This book relies on Laurence's own truths, but also calls on the gifts and experiences I had in following her spiritual journey. I started the project with some trepidation, for she was an icon whom many readers and scholars felt they knew. As more biographies were published, I wondered what I could add, but I kept following my instinct, trying to divine the well I'd sensed when we met in 1978. When I finally started writing, I began to dream about her. In the first dream, her friend Alice Olsen Williams, whom I'd just interviewed, and I met Laurence in a farmhouse kitchen, then drove her somewhere. When we dropped Laurence off, I knew she was skeptical of what I was doing, but wasn't going to stop me. I then was working late in my den one summer night, trying to decipher the connection between her African and Canadian writing, when I felt her standing behind my left shoulder, satisfied with the links I was drawing from the path she'd left behind. Finally, the week I finished writing this book, I had a dream that ended with her inviting me to stay in her Lakefield home as she left for church. I was relieved, feeling I'd navigated safely through her sacred ground and finally gained her blessing.

There have been many blessings in writing this book. I've learned from the wisdom of Laurence's journey and her wonderful friends who shared parts of her story with me. I've also plumbed the depths of my soul to finally begin to answer my call and write what I most value. Margaret Laurence's life and work were a gift of grace, and we, her inheritors, are still being blessed by them. This is her story, with the lessons I've learned documented in the end. But, she also passed the torch to a new generation, which now presents us, her inheritors, with a valuable opportunity to consider how we can honour her legacy by answering our own spiritual calls and serving our communities.

CHAPTER 2

GROWING UP PRAIRIE

When Margaret Laurence was born in the old Neepawa General Hospital on July 18, 1926, she was called Jean Margaret Wemyss. Her parents were still young people in love, and their families were part of the town's elite. Laurence's dad, Robert Wemyss, was a local lawyer and her mother, Verna (Simpson) Wemyss, was an amateur pianist. Both families were deeply rooted in this Canadian prairie community that always remained part of Laurence's soul.

Neepawa, Manitoba, was then a beautifully treed town of 1,800 people, located about 150 kilometres northwest of Winnipeg. The pioneers had cut it from the bush fifty years earlier, but were still part of its fabric, far more than the Native tribes who had roamed the area for two centuries. The town was set amid fertile fields, but didn't look like flat prairie as its gentle roll rose in a steep hill into town and the low Riding Mountains framed it to the north. There was so much poplar and spruce that it appeared to be more parkland than prairie, but the people prided themselves on being prairie. I knew because I came from the town immediately west, and my dad was born a year after Laurence in the village due east, the third of five generations to live there. The people in our communities may have been town's folk, but they were still attuned to the land's rhythm and agricultural service sector that their grandparents forged with hard work and co-operation.

By the time Laurence was born, Neepawa had an established personality that wove together both enterprise and co-operation, a blend that deeply influenced her foundation. In 1926, the town was a strong, but still growing centre that served the surrounding agricultural district. It had a few wooden homes, but many buildings were made of brick from the brick yard north of town. The town's core was well established with a post office, court house, churches, banks, hotels, and even the current newspaper, *The Neepawa Press*. The new Neepawa Salt Company was mining salt and the hospital was adding a wing. Within three years, the Viscount School that Laurence attended was constructed and the Roxy Theatre started showing "talkies." Despite the Depression, a new arena and meat plant were also erected by 1935. What was less obvious was the town's strong co-operative base. Not only did people band together to survive the harsh elements, but their community's prosperity was anchored by co-operatives. Eight farm families owned their own phone company for twenty years, and the local farmers decided to save on goods by launching the Neepawa Consumers Co-op at a 1929

Manitoba Pool Elevator meeting. This was a culture that honoured both free enterprise and co-operativism, leaving its people with a sense of adventurous free will but also the importance of working together to achieve their ends.

This interesting blend also played out in Neepawa's politics. Provincially, its people tended to vote Conservative, but during Laurence's time there—from 1926 to 1944—it elected a member from the populist prairie-based Progressive party in 1927 before returning a Conservative member in 1936. Nationally, it see-sawed between the two until it elected Conservative druggist Tom Murphy in 1930. He became part of Prime Minister R.B. Bennett's cabinet, which named Laurence's beloved vacation area around Clear Lake as the Riding Mountain National Park. But that government did little to help Neepawa during the Depression when transients were knocking on doors, looking for handouts, and sometimes working on threshing gangs. A Mackenzie King Liberal finally defeated Murphy in 1935 when the Conservatives fell, but not before Laurence grew to hate Bennett. Documentary writer Bill Whitehead saw that in the 1970s after he inherited some money that Bennett left Whitehead's family. Bill used the money to install a swimming pool in the backyard of the farm north of Toronto that he shared with his partner, Timothy Findley. The couple jokingly told a few friends how the pool was financed, and one day, while they were picking up Laurence for a weekend visit at the farm, a colleague planted a professionally painted sign that said "The R.B. Bennett Memorial Pool" beside it. When they returned with Laurence, Whitehead laughed: "She took one look at the sign and insisted 'take me home.' She refused to have anything to do with the name of the man whose economic policies she blamed for the Great Depression. Fortunately, she was finally persuaded to stay—but not to change her opinion of our former Prime Minister."[1]

Laurence's family on both her mother's and father's sides helped to shape Neepawa. Her paternal grandfather, John Wemyss, studied in Edinburgh before moving to Neepawa in 1887, where he became its first resident lawyer and served on many boards, including that of Knox Presbyterian Church. He died of a heart attack a month after Laurence was born, which she always regretted since he was probably the only one in town who could read the ancient Greek plays that she later found among his books. John married Maggie, the daughter of Neepawa's first banker, Dr. D.H. Harrison, a retired Ontario doctor who was briefly Manitoba's premier in the late 1880s. Their son, Robert—Laurence's dad—became a partner in his father's law firm. Laurence's maternal grandfather was John Simpson, the son of Irish immigrants who settled in Ontario. He moved to Neepawa in 1890, where he bought a furniture store, developed a hardware store, then started the Simpson and Son Funeral Home in 1896, which remained in the family until his son died in 1935. Simpson was a grumpy old man by the time Laurence was born, but he was also a staunch Methodist and a member of the Oddfellows, Shriners, and Masonic Lodge. He married Jane Bailey, whose family were United Empire Loyalists, also from Ontario.

When Laurence grew up, she became aware of Neepawa's class differences, which were drawn along ethnic lines. While the town had Scots, Irish, English, and Ukrainian residents, she remembered that the Scots and Ukrainians were the two largest groups and the well-educated Scots professionals, her class, looked down on the Ukrainian peasant farmers who worked for the railways.[2] She remembered being so brainwashed as a child—"not by our parents particularly but by the stratified society in which we had grown up"—that she and her friend, Mona, tried to get the attention of a Ukrainian boy from the other side of the tracks who was repairing their house by chanting, "in a horrifying way. 'Hunky, hunky, hunky.'" He scolded them and she never did that again.[3] The class differences eventually became so marked that Laurence said in a 1981 interview: "I am very much aware, as I was even when I was a young person in my home town, that there are people who lead difficult, impoverished lives, people who were and still are oppressed."[4]

Laurence spent half of her Neepawa years living with her Irish Methodist relatives, but she was deeply imprinted by her dad's family's Scottish Presbyterianism. She recalled growing up in a rigid Scots-Irish background of stern values, hard work, and puritanism, but later said, "I had been brought up with a very strong knowledge of my Scottish background."[5] She learned Scottish songs as a child, wore a gold Scottish seal-ring with the Wemyss insignia, and found the bagpipes her "soul music" when she sat on the steps listening to an elderly neighbour play them in his back yard. She was even intrigued by a Scottish great-aunt, Ettie, who occasionally visited, and had a thick accent and a habit of eating porridge by dipping a spoonful of oatmeal into a cup of cold milk. Laurence later tried to trace her Scottish heritage while she was living overseas, but she found that it only led her back to the Scottish roots that she developed in Neepawa.

It's difficult from this distance to know exactly what Laurence learned about religion in her formative years. But, being from rural Manitoba, I know how important the church was to a small town then, and her views of organized religion and her struggle with it were influenced by what she learned from her church and her family. She was only five months old when she was baptized in the United Church, the new denomination that was formed when the Presbyterian, Methodist, and Congregational churches amalgamated in 1925. Like most children then, she attended Sunday school, where she was remembered for her giggling, was briefly in the teen girls' group called the Canadian Girls in Training, and played violin in the small Sunday school orchestra. She even rewrote a Christmas play for the "Sunbeams" Sunday school class when its leader, her high-school French teacher Connie Offen, couldn't find a play with enough parts for all of its six-year-olds. Laurence said in her memoir that her step-mum also "counted herself a Christian," but wasn't as flamboyant as one of their hired girls, a young Salvation Army woman, who used to belt out "Will Your Anchor Hold." Laurence's maternal grandmother, Jane Simpson, was also a "very religious person" who "quite simply lived by her faith." She gave Laurence a King James Bible in 1935, just after Laurence's dad died. Laurence loved its poetry and recalled:

> Grandmother gave me my first (and indeed only) Bible....
> I have carried it around the world with me for more than
> fifty years. It is tattered now, and the soft black leather
> cover is held together with tape. It is full of pen markings,
> where I have noted passages I wanted to be able to find
> again easily. In fact, it's the only Bible in which I can find
> anything. I think of my grandmother whenever I open it.[6]

Laurence didn't go to church much as an adult, but her prairie religious background etched a deep groove in her life and work. She told *Chatelaine* in 1971 that she was grounded by her family's Scottish Presbyterianism, where "we absorbed our religion more in the moral terms than theological. The virtuous person is he who works hard."[7] As an adult, she often labelled her feelings of guilt or repression as

Scottish Presbyterianism, but also retained a deep love of the old hymns and carols. As she wrote ex-Manitoban writer Gabrielle Roy in 1977, she was moved to tears when the audience was invited to sing the beloved carols—including her favourite, "It Came Upon a Midnight Clear"—at the Royal Choral Society's Christmas concert in London the previous Christmas. "Are the words really as beautiful and as moving as I think, or do I invest them with all the emotional impact of a lifetime? I don't think it matters." She sang her heart out, hardly able to see the words for tears, but added, "[T]hat was all right.... I knew the words anyway. I thought of the hymn we call Old Hundred.... All people that on earth do dwell."[8] She incorporated that Old Hundred hymn in her fiction and asked to have it sung at her funeral.

CHAPTER 3

THE ROAD TO THE BIG HOUSE

Laurence recalled her childhood as basically happy, but it was more traumatic than most. By the time she was ten, her mother, dad, uncle, and Grandmother Simpson had died, and she'd moved several times, though always in Neepawa. She ended up in her Grandfather Simpson's home, the blond brick house at 312 First Avenue, which is now Neepawa's primary attraction, the Margaret Laurence Home. It is located near the north end of the downtown's main street and was also portrayed as the Connor house in her book of short stories, *A Bird in the House*.

Laurence's only memory of her birth mother occurred in that house. Verna Wemyss was the second youngest of the Simpson children and a high-spirited woman, but she was ill at the time of Laurence's memory, which was right after her fourth birthday party. Marg, Verna's older sister, helped Laurence tug her new trike up the back stairs and Laurence later recalled: "I happily run to my mother, excitedly telling her about the new trike.... My mother, lying in the grey-painted double bed, smiles at me. Her face is white, and her dark hair is spread out across the white pillowcase. She touches my face, my hair."[1] Verna died two days later. Laurence thought it was from a kidney infection, but biographer Lyall Powers said in *Alien Heart* that it was peritonitis following a sudden appendicitis attack that she had after Laurence's birthday party. Word spread quickly and a playmate told Laurence before her family could break the news to her.

Laurence's Aunt Marg, who soon became her "Mum," stepped in to care for her namesake and became a potent force in her life. Aunt Marg was a tall, slender intellectual who'd graduated from high school with Manitoba's highest marks. But her father, John Simpson, wouldn't let her go to university because he didn't believe in educating women. Marg taught in Bermuda on an exchange for a year before moving to Calgary to teach high school. She was home for the summer, but never went back. Aunt Marg soon moved in with her brother-in-law, Robert, staying at the "Little House" that he and Verna built at 265 Vivian Street before they married. Laurence thought Marg slept in the back room for a year until they were married in Brandon in 1931. Marg was forty-one and Robert thirty-seven, and they adopted baby Robert in 1933.

Laurence had eight good years with her dad before he died on January 13, 1935. He had the reputation of being a bit of a hellion who had to finish high school in a private Toronto boys' academy. He articled in Winnipeg, served in World War I with his brother—whom he accidentally shot with a BB gun as a child, blinding him in one eye—then became his dad's law partner. Robert loved gardening and carpentry, and built Laurence a large playhouse, complete with window boxes filled with flowers. The family spent eighteen months at his parents' place—the Wemyss' House at 483 Second Avenue—after his mom moved to Winnipeg, but the young family moved back to the Little House just before Robert died of pneumonia. Laurence always believed his death resulted from a flu epidemic since her mum's brother, undertaker Stuart Simpson, died of pneumonia a week later. But when I talked to the townsfolk, they said the men's pneumonia followed some late-night revelry. The town's professionals were poor then, but often had parties. The Wemysses were walking home drunk one cold January night when Robert fell a few houses north of his house. Marg couldn't get him up, so left him and went home. Laurence said he was only sick for a few days, but one night she felt so uneasy that she slept with her mum in the guest room while the doctors tended her dad: "When I woke up in the middle of the night, my mother was crying, and I knew my father was dead."[2]

The loss was devastating and Laurence recalled wearing a surly, angry mask, her only defence against crying. She also empathized with her mum, married only three years and left with her, aged eight, and Bob, not quite two. Laurence's childhood friend, Louise (Alguire) Kubik, remembered seeing Laurence in the Simpson house after her dad died: "I was dressed up, and there was Peggy all dressed up and receiving people." It was even more devastating after Laurence's Grandmother Simpson died at age seventy-seven the following May. The small Wemyss family moved into the "Big House" for "reasons of practicality and finances." She said:

> I felt very odd about that move. I had loved that house all my life, but it was for visiting, not for living in. It was my grandfather's stronghold and he ruled it like Agamemnon ruling Mycenae or Jehovah ruling the world. It had its secret corners, its fascinations, but it was his domain, not mine. It did become mine, in time. We moved there when I was ten and it was where I lived until I left home for college, eight years later. In fact when I think of my childhood home, it is that one more than any other that comes to mind.[3]

CHAPTER 4

A WRITER'S SENSIBILITIES

Laurence had mixed memories of the town that shaped her way of seeing the world. It was a warm, protective atmosphere, almost like an extended family since everyone knew everyone else. But it also felt stultifying because there were so few who shared her interests. She was middle-aged before she made some peace with it, even though it had already left its imprint.

While Laurence remembered being a lonely child, she actually had a strong community of friends, a pattern she often repeated as an adult. Milkman Bert Batchelor's daughter, Dorothy Brown, told me that Laurence and her friends used to wait outside her house until he hooked her sled to his horse-drawn wagon and pulled them around. Laurence also knew Mona (Spratt) Meredith from the time they were toddlers and they remained friends most of their lives. By the time she was ten, Laurence had two friends her age, Meredith and Margie Crawford, and Kubik, a year younger. In high school, her circle expanded to include the three other girls in her senior class. Kubik remembered their parents' circle also included the

Wemysses, Spratts, and Alguires. "Our mothers were best friends," she said. "The ladies played bridge and Mah Jong. Aunt Marg was a whiz at counting." But, Meredith recalled that group didn't always involve Marg after her husband died.

The girls played kids' stuff, but some of it fed Laurence's earliest career choice of nursing. It was the days of radio serials, so they had Little Orphan Annie badges and rings, and made up secret codes. They also had sleepovers and went to Saturday afternoon movies. But the hospital superintendent gave Laurence a first aid kit, and Laurence also set up an apothecary's shop in the garage loft and grew and dried herbs for it. Her mum gave her a microscope, so Laurence and Meredith used to prick their fingers to study their blood on the glass slides.

Laurence was never athletic, so did not participate any more than she had to in most sports, but she loved being outdoors where she could play and enjoy being in nature. She said it helped form the "sight of my eyes," which was one of the two wellsprings for her writing, the other being her own experience. She loved the cottage her dad built in the 1920s at Clear Lake in the Riding Mountain National Park, which was fifty kilometres north and the place where he also taught her to swim. She enjoyed curling, and she and her friends snowshoed, played tennis, and rode their bikes miles to visit their friends in the neighbouring towns of Arden and Franklin. They also loved to skate. They'd clear snow from the river, where they kept long boards to rescue kids who fell in. Once the new arena was built, they used to skate there three nights a week and sometimes meet boys. She later said it all contributed to her sense of place:

> I can remember the physical appearance of things, so that when I'm writing about Southern Manitoba I am able to see it in my mind extremely clearly. Partly it's because when you're a child the physical environment makes a very strong impact on you, although you don't recognize it at the time. As a child you look at things very carefully, you notice a great many things about the environment and the country that you wouldn't notice later on. The country, the land is, after all, very close to a small town; it's just beyond the brow of the town hill. So that, although I didn't actually ever live on a farm I lived very close to open country. When we were kids we used to visit and play there and bicycle out to the country a great deal, and this stands out in my memory.[1]

Laurence's Neepawa years also brought her the gift of music, which not only tied her closer to her community but became important to her later writing. Given that her birth mother was a pianist, her step-mum made her study piano, which she hated, then let her learn violin. Laurence played in the school orchestra for three years—a small band of six to nine students that usually had a piano, drums, wind or string instruments, and occasionally a guitar. It played for school events, church potlucks, and even fowl suppers. By then, her music was starting to augment her sense of place and spirit. In a later essay she described how her family attended the Christmas Eve service and sang carols, including one of her favourites, "It Came Upon a Midnight Clear":

> It couldn't have been even near midnight when we walked home after those services, but it always seemed to me that I knew exactly what "midnight clear" meant. I had no sense then that there could be any kind of winter other than ours. It was a prairie town, and by Christmas the snow would always be thick and heavy, yet light and clean as well, something to be battled against and respected when it fell in blinding blizzards, but also something which created an upsurge of the heart at times such as those, walking back home on Christmas Eve with the carols still echoing in your head. The evening would be still, almost silent, and the air would be so dry and sharp you could practically touch the coldness. The snow would be dark-shadowed and then suddenly it would look like sprinkled rainbows around the sparse streetlights. Sometimes there were northern lights ... a blazing eerie splendor across the sky, swift-moving, gigantic, like a message. It was easy then to believe in the Word made manifest. Not so easy now. And yet I can't forget, ever, that the child, who was myself then, experienced awe and recognized it.[2]

CHAPTER 5

THE MASK OF THE BEAR

By the time Laurence moved into her Grandfather John Simpson's Big House in 1936, he was eighty and a hard man who'd had a challenging life. He was born in Milton, Ontario, the youngest of six, but he quit school at twelve to become an apprentice cabinetmaker. His dad died when John was fourteen, so the young lad had to help support his family. He left for Manitoba in 1877 and travelled by sternwheeler and train. Short of funds, he walked the last hundred kilometres to Portage la Prairie, where he worked with his cousin in a men's clothing store. He married Jane Bailey in 1886 and they had two children in two years, but a fire destroyed their apartment above the store. They jumped to safety, but moved to Neepawa in 1890, where he developed his businesses, then passed his funeral home to his reluctant eldest son, Stuart, who would rather have been a lawyer than an undertaker in his dad's company.

Simpson was shrewd and successful, but a difficult man. He angrily thumped around the house, reducing everyone with his fury. He scowled at anyone who sat in his padded church pew, and shook his fist at any children who dared to cut across his lawn. One person remembered him paying someone he hired for the day with a child's casket, and Laurence's friends recalled he was a gruff, mean man with steely eyes. Mona (Spratt) Meredith, Laurence's best friend from childhood, told me: "[T]he kids could never do anything right. None of us could."

Given his disposition, it's little wonder that Laurence struggled with his memory for most of her life. She described him as a stern, authoritarian father, domineering husband, and irascible old man who couldn't show affection, except for the time that he greeted her, crying, when his wife died. She hated and feared him, and recalled him raging for days when he found candle stubs in the garage loft. Kubik said Laurence once invited her to dinner because Laurence's mum was going out and Laurence had to cook for him: "She had to fry meat and she'd flip it over and say, 'Burn.'"

Laurence was a budding writer who found this atmosphere difficult. She'd always had a vivid imagination, starting stories at three with "Once upon a time."[1] She remembered telling herself tales as a child, then constantly writing poetry, funny verses, stories, and "once a highly uninformed but jubilantly imaginative journal of Captain John Ball and his voyages to exotic lands."[2] She traced her writing career back to Grade 2, but a classmate remembered her writing a story about their

Clear Lake holiday when she was six, then asking neighbours if they wanted to hear it for a penny, and several agreed. Another classmate said their elementary class was on a nature hike in a pasture east of town when the teacher noticed Laurence was missing and sent two children back to find her. She was sitting under an oak tree, her scribbler in her lap, writing.

One of the difficulties of living with her grandfather was that she always needed "an unusual amount of privacy in order to think and write."[3] When she still lived in her first house, she could go to her attic bedroom and write on the turquoise desk that her father had given her. But once she moved in with her grandfather, she needed a refuge, as he thought she was wasting her time writing. Her mum put a little table in her bedroom, but Laurence escaped to the play-house that her dad had built and her mum had brought with them. She'd even go in winter, "to brood upon life's injustices, to work off anger, or simply to think and dream."[4] In summer, she'd climb onto its roof to read, hidden by the spruce branches. Then, she found the garage loft was the best place to hide from prying eyes in the summer: "I used to cheat on my violin practice and whip up to the loft, where I kept my five-cent scribblers in which I was writing a novel entitled *The Pillars of the Nation*." She soon quit her violin lessons because she was only interested in writing.

Laurence had a spiritual experience about her writing when she was fourteen. She was walking up the stairs to her bedroom in her grandfather's house when a thought came to her "with enormous strength: I can't be a nurse; I have to be a writer. I was appalled and frightened.... What frightened me was not the writing itself.... No, what scared me was how, if I wasn't going to be a nurse, I would earn a living."[5] When Lois (Freeman) Wilson, a later friend who became Moderator of The United Church of Canada, asked her during a dialogue at Kingston's Chalmers United Church in 1979 whether she experienced a "call" to write, Laurence replied:

> I really think that almost all serious writers, if they really continue, experience a sense of vocation. When young writers say, "Do you think I should be a writer," I say if you don't *have* to be, then don't do it. It's something that you feel as a sense of vocation; you simply cannot imagine yourself doing anything else. And you have to have that deep sense of really lifetime commitment to this. I think that in some ways it's really similar to the ministry.[6]

The call marked Laurence's efforts to start publishing. That year, when she visited her Aunt Ruby, who was a nursing director in Regina, Laurence had her aunt's secretary type her story—which Laurence called *Pillars of the Nation*, but Powers discovered was *The Land of Our Fathers*. She submitted it to the *Winnipeg Free Press*'s summer contest for young authors and won an honourable mention in September 1940.

While Laurence was in Grade 9 in the same year, she also submitted *The Case of the Blond Butcher* to the *Free Press*, and the girl's detective story with a romantic twist was published by the newspaper in January 1941.

Laurence had two Neepawa women who encouraged her writing. One was her mum, Marg, whose first love was English literature. Once Laurence was allowed to stop taking music lessons, she said her mum realized that writing "might be the important area of my spirit" where "she could help me the most and, over many years, she did." Their house was full of books, which her mum encouraged her to read, and even though Laurence liked adventure stories best, Marg gave her Willa Cather's books and *Paradise Lost* to read. They then discussed her reading and took turns while they were doing dishes to see who could go the furthest in quoting poetry. Marg paid half the cost of Laurence's fourteen-dollar typewriter, while Laurence paid the other half by babysitting. Marg also provided tactful criticism and honest praise for Laurence's writing and encouraged her to write what she knew, rather than about lords and ladies in ancient castles.

Marg's post as the town's first librarian also influenced Laurence. Two local reading circles started working to establish Neepawa's public library in 1937, and after meeting with the Dauphin librarian, they formed a board, wrote a constitution, and named Marg the librarian. When the library eventually opened, it began by charging members three dollars a year and borrowing books from Dauphin. It also accepted donations and bought second-hand books. Marg was interested in Canadian literature, so she and Laurence pored over the *Quill & Quire*, trying to get the most books for the least money. Laurence read the latest Canadian fiction, including Sinclair Ross's *As For Me and My House* in 1941, which she later said in an interview confirmed what her mum had been telling her—to write what she knew: "[F]or years, I thought, well, what I know is this town, who wants to read about that?" "Then I read *As For Me and My House* and ... it was like a revelation. I thought, 'I come from a small little town like this and I can write. I don't have to live in Toronto.' I would say that was a turning point in my early life as a writer ... it gave me the sense that I could write out of my own background."[7]

One cannot emphasize how important that was because when I grew up in the next town twenty-five years later, there was no public library. We borrowed books mailed from Winnipeg's extension service. I'd carefully comb its catalogue for my selections, then, months later, receive completely different books. By junior high, we could buy Scholastic and TAB paperbacks at school, and I saved my allowance to buy Nancy Drew books in Winnipeg. But I, like most rural kids, never knew there was a Canadian literature until I got to university in the 1970s.

Laurence's other key influence was Mildred Musgrove, who taught her high-school English and typing and was staff advisor for the student paper that Laurence edited. Laurence later recalled that the "chief joys of high school, and they remained so for four years, were being able to work on the school newspaper and studying English literature."[8] She liked composition, and when she studied British literature in Grade 11, she felt as though a series of doors were opening in her mind. She read Keats, Wordsworth, and Shelley, but later noted that Browning's "incredible dramatic monologues," such as *My Last Duchess*, "probably did influence me greatly, in a fascination with the portrayal of a human individual."[9] When Laurence was in Grade 12, she also studied Shakespeare and the Bible, which later influenced her writing, too.

Many still comment on how crusty Musgrove was, but she encouraged Laurence's writing. When Musgrove retired in 1969, Laurence wrote to her to say how much Musgrove had influenced her, and some of the ways were similar to those in which Laurence's mum also encouraged her. "I still remember the way you taught Browning in Grade Eleven," she wrote Musgrove, "and how it seemed to me like a kind of fantastic discovery. And I remember when I edited the highschool paper, and how much I appreciated working with you on that. Perhaps most of all, I remember how you gave me realistic and yet never-damaging criticisms of my poems and stories —the sort of criticism that a young person desperately needs, the sort of positive criticism which can encourage a beginning writer to go on and to discover more about the craft of writing." It was a powerful support for the young woman who would become one of Canada's most famous writers, and one that she would eventually pass on to the young people that she later met.

CHAPTER 6

HIGH-SCHOOL JOURNALISM

Once Laurence felt the call to be a writer, she assumed she'd make her living in journalism. That assumption remained throughout her schooling, but she started her career on Neepawa's high-school paper in Grade 10 by contributing a story for the Christmas 1941 issue. "Goodwill Towards Men" was the tale of a Scottish boy who captured a German paratrooper on Christmas Eve, and it had many religious references—the boy returned from church and sang hymns to comfort himself, and his mother hoped peace would come: "Because a baby was born in a stable in Bethlehem." Laurence also wrote articles about the school dance and orchestra later that year.

When she became the paper's editor in the fall of 1942, Laurence worked with Musgrove, her French teacher Connie Offen, and a committee, but enthusiastically encouraged others to submit reports for the quarterly. She also started some advocacy journalism about World War II, urging students to take an interest in the new world that was unfolding. That might seem surprising in someone so young, but it flowed from her feeling that the war transformed her life. She later wrote: "[O]n September 5, 1939, my world changed out of all recognition, forever. It had not been an idyllic world. It had had its terrors, its nightmares, but compared with the world in which my children grew up, it had been a small and rural world, upon which the vast outside impinged relatively little. That simplicity would never be possible again."[1]

The war's effect on Laurence started small, but steadily mounted. In 1940, the Dominion government's *War Measures Act* required anyone aged sixteen and over to register in case they were needed in a national emergency. In June 1941, Germany invaded Russia, and fifteen months later, there were only two boys in her Grade 11 class; by Grade 12, there were none. Her first boyfriend, Don Straith, a farm boy two years older whom she had dated for two years, joined the Royal Canadian Air Force. Her second cousin, Lorne Bailey, a farm boy from north of Neepawa, also enlisted. In 1944, her friend Bob, who was the first person to tell her when the war was declared, also died in a burning tank during the Canadian army's final European campaign against the Nazis.

The biggest impact, however, was when about two-thirds of the Canadians who charged Dieppe on August 19, 1942 were killed, wounded, or captured. Many of Neepawa's boys, who were in the Queen's Own Cameron Highlanders, died in that assault. As she later wrote in her memoir:

I was sixteen that year, and for the first time I knew, really knew, what war meant. It meant that young men from your own town, your friends or brothers of your friends, boys only a couple of years older than yourself, had been mutilated and killed. Boys of eighteen, nineteen, twenty years old. I think it was only through that knowledge that all the other dead and suffering people from all the wars became finally and forever real to me. Before, despite my father's experience, they had been appalling statistics, but they were not statistics any more. They were boys I had known. They were a part of me.[2]

Laurence did what she could for the war effort while she was in school. Musgrove noted in her speech to open Neepawa's Manawaka Gallery in 1983 that "Margaret vigorously promoted both school and national spirit during a time of war. Peggy's editorials were often pleas to buy war savings stamps or to collect rags and paper. Do any of you remember how cold and dirty was the old United Church stable where we bundled and sorted paper, or how sordid the task of packing rags?" Laurence's personal focus was promoting War Savings Stamps, but she championed the school's War Services Committee's work and the students collected 952 pounds of salvage in 1944. They used clothes for rags and wool to make Red Cross blankets, and the boys loaded scrap iron, rubber, and paper to ship, and tin foil and aluminum pots to melt. In her last editorial in 1944, Laurence noted that the war couldn't, as some thought, be won on the home front, but it was important to buy war bonds, gather salvage, and knit for the Red Cross: "If our part is small, let us play it cheerfully, humbly, and to the very best of our ability."

Laurence's editorials were sometimes even more idealistic. The *Neepawa Press* was regularly carrying war news—the names of the dead, wounded, and missing, weekly accounts of the war and local training school, and ads for war bonds, the Red Cross, and salvage collection—so she urged students to consider their place in the new world. In December 1942, she wrote: "Today more than ever before, students in the free countries of the world should be working to the best of their ability, and endeavoring to make themselves fit to be citizens of their country. Remember that it is you and I—the students of today, whose task it will be to build up the world after the war." In her last 1944 editorial, she even foreshadowed speeches she gave toward the end of her life. She wrote that while Canadians had been able to live in a free and peaceful world, they had a responsibility to others since only a few of the world's youth had the same privilege:

> It is because of this tremendous debt to our country that we may have to help here more in the future. It is also because others have not been so fortunate as we. All mankind is curiously bound to one another, whether we

like it or not. There is no real isolation policy, because no one can be a law unto himself. One downtrodden race is the business of everyone in the whole world.... Therefore the responsibility for this war cannot be shifted to the shoulders of anyone else. It is our business.[3]

CHAPTER 7

GRADUATION: AN ERA ENDS

Laurence's high-school years went well, but she was ready for college. She'd debated and played lead in the school drama production, but was best known for her untiring newspaper work. She saw herself as a shy, nervous girl who was often depressed, but she earned the reputation of being an enthusiastic leader and outgoing friend. In 1943, at the end of Grade 11, she won the Governor-General's Medal and spent the summer working as the *Neepawa Press*'s district news editor, compiling family news from the surrounding areas. She stayed in town to finish Grade 12, which was the equivalent of a first year Bachelor of Arts, but cheaper than university.

Laurence and her friends wanted to leave Neepawa. They were eager to see the world, but even more keen to abandon the town's narrowness. Laurence had seen that trait in the petty comments that some women made when her mum married, telling her that a green wedding dress was unlucky and a Christian man shouldn't marry his dead wife's sister. As teens, Meredith told me, the young women were driven crazy when they put on lipstick after they left the house and "somebody would see that and go home and phone your mother and tell her, 'Did you know your daughter has lipstick on?'" It was too much to have everyone knowing their business, and as Laurence later said: "I wanted to get out—almost everybody at that age wants to get out."[1]

Laurence's first escape plan was to join the Women's Royal Canadian Naval Service, but she was relieved when she missed the phone call telling her she was admitted. She decided then that she'd never liked joining organizations and she was really "a prairie person in every bone."[2]

She applied for a Manitoba scholarship so she could afford to go to college. The small Wemyss family was not as hard up as some in the Depression, but it had little money and Laurence remembered her mum being constantly worried. Her friend Meredith added that Laurence's family continued to scrimp through the war years, and while she thought Marg had sold her husband's law firm, Grandfather Simpson wasn't as financially well off as others believed since the person who bought his business did not finish paying him. Marg tried to make ends meet by taking in a boarder, but her family hated it, so she never did that again. Laurence, like many rural Manitobans, sometimes had to wear hand-me-downs—though hers came from the doctor's daughter—but she detested it so much that she worked for Leckie's Ladies Wear Saturdays during high school so that she could buy dresses and satin underwear. She finally won the scholarship and was accepted into Winnipeg's United College. "The doors to the world were opening," she wrote in her memoir, noting that Meredith was going to the University of Manitoba. "As we contemplated our futures, we both felt a touching combination of bravado and fear."[3]

CHAPTER 8

WINNIPEG'S UNITED COLLEGE

When Laurence, then still known as Peggy Wemyss, arrived in Winnipeg in the fall of 1944, she was ready to embrace a new life and she picked the right place to do it. United College was the United Church's liberal arts school, which was affiliated with the University of Manitoba (U. of M.) in the 1940s before the college became the University of Winnipeg in 1967. United College was founded when the Methodist Wesley College and Presbyterian Manitoba College amalgamated in 1938. These founding colleges had already educated such prominent, progressive Manitobans as J.S. Woodsworth, who formed the NDP's forerunner, the CCF, and Stanley Knowles, who became a long-serving CCF, then NDP, Member of Parliament.

Manitoba's capital had 220,000 people, and the grey castle-like college stood on the western edge of downtown. Meredith started studying interior decorating and Kubik took home economics at the U. of M.'s Fort Garry campus, a half-hour streetcar ride south, but Meredith lived at the Y near United

College the first year, so the friends met for Saturday movies. Laurence's other chum, Margie Crawford, enrolled in science at United College, so Laurence didn't know a soul when she started the second year of her B.A. program, with English, history, ethics, psychology, French, and German classes.

It wasn't long before she began to build community, first with other residence students, such as her roommate Helen (Warkentin) Stanley, then with Madge Hetherington from Carman and Mary (Turnbull) Mindess from Winnipeg. Laurence avoided sororities because of her strong egalitarian views, but also because she couldn't afford them and wasn't interested in tea parties. Since United was a small institution with twenty professors and about five hundred students, classes were small and students got to know each other and their professors. Laurence later said: "This was the first time in my life that I found a number of different people who shared my interests, with whom I could communicate them. There'd been a few in my home town but, for the first time, there were *quite* a few."[1] One of her biographers, Lyall Powers, who went to college with her, said a group of the students—including Laurence, Mindess, and Jack Borland, whom she dated—used to share their writing and discuss literature, and Patricia (Jenkins) Blondal sometimes joined them. Blondal later had two novels posthumously published. The most notable was *A Candle To Light the Sun*, which was released in 1960, just months after she died of cancer in late 1959.

It is interesting to hear how people viewed Laurence as a college student because it reflected not only how she'd seen herself in high school, but also how she was often described later. They routinely said that she was shy, quiet, insecure, and even aloof until she started debating issues about which she was passionate. Then she could be brash and enthusiastic about literature, the purpose of religion, or ways to achieve social justice. She'd stomp about residence singing at the top of her lungs, and her roommate, Stanley, said that Laurence "seemed freer and more independent of mind than the rest of us."[2] John and Angela (Baird) Graham, older students at United College who also later knew her in London, Ontario, noted how singularly focused she was on writing, never joining the drama club or debating team. Gerald Bedford, another college friend, recalled that she was an intense, persistent, and intelligent young woman who was interested in the poor and finding solutions to problems. He thought she smoked, drank, and sat up late talking in order to reject tradition. "If you knew her then, you'd have thought she was anti-religious and very secular," he told me. "But she felt very strongly about everything, including the Bible."

College life had its ups and downs. When Laurence wrote to her high-school paper that fall, she said someone had stuffed a goat in a boys' room, then took it to the girls' residence, and it took several of them to get it out. There was also a lot of water-bombing. She remembered being water-bombed for reciting Shelley's poetry too loudly on the residence fire escape, but classmate Lois (Freeman) Wilson, the Dean of Theology's daughter, recalled several of them—including Laurence—tossing paper bags of water from the college's third-floor windows as students entered below. Laurence also found the lectures interesting, but harder to assimilate than high school, and she wrote her former classmates: "I was decidedly startled to discover that it was necessary to work much, much harder than I had ever done before."[3] She got her best mark in ethics that year, but failed history. She spent that summer studying history in Neepawa so she could retest in August. As she wrote Stanley after she got her failing history mark that spring: "I thought of not going back to U.C. next year, but I'd hate not going back worse than going back." She also took breaks during her summer studies to draw a modern art mural called "Evolution," which had primitively drawn waves, amoebas, palm trees, and red and purple dinosaurs as she worked up to Adam and Eve. She used it to brighten her and Stanley's sparsely decorated room.

One of the noteworthy items from that summer was the kind of detail Laurence included in her letters, for they already had the portrait quality for which she later became known. In mid-May, she wrote her college roommate, Helen (Warkentin) Stanley: "Right now I'm sitting on the back yard, on the lawn, leaning against a maple tree. It is warm & sunny, & the birds are singing like everything. The garden hasn't been planted yet but it's ploughed, & the earth looks clean in the sunlight. Just ahead of me is a line of spruces & to my right is the garden & the fence—rather weatherbeaten & full of missing boards." She added details as people passed, then: "Grandfather has just come stomping out to get some wood, saying rather nastily 'what in the world are you doing there?' I considered telling him I was writing a book on Pantheism, but upon reflection decided that perhaps nature study is not in his vocabulary. He is supposed to be sick in bed with a lame knee, but apparently believing his granddaughter to be crazy beyond all possible redemption, he rose with a fine early Christian martyr attitude to light the fire. Ah grandfathers."

United College strongly influenced Laurence in two key areas—literature and the social gospel. She majored in English literature and especially appreciated two professors with whom she maintained contact. One was Robert Hallstead, an American hired in 1946 as more veterans returned to college. She liked his enthusiasm for writing and studying literature, and his interest in humane causes. The other was Dr. Malcolm Ross, who taught Milton and seventeenth-century English thought at the U. of M. He later published her first "real" story in *Queen's Quarterly*, then several of her books in McClelland and Stewart's New Canadian Library. She said both men encouraged her in the same way that her mum and Musgrove had: "These people were not giving me an unthinking or uncritical encouragement ... they were critical, always, but always in a constructive way that helped me to examine my work and try to do better."[4]

Laurence joined the English Club, which met monthly at Professor Arthur Phelps' house. It was meant for senior students, which she didn't know when she asked to join, but Phelps agreed, then warned the others to be courteous to her. He encouraged students to read Canadian fiction, and Laurence recalled reading books by such writers as Morley Callaghan, Gabrielle Roy, and Hugh MacLennan in the nearby Hudson Bay's book department because "we couldn't afford to buy them, and they weren't even greatly in evidence at the Public Library."[5] The club, which usually involved students discussing a paper that one of them presented on an aspect of English literature, was one of her happiest and most rewarding college experiences, but it also augmented her schooling. York University professor Clara Thomas, who wrote many books and articles on Laurence's work, said in *Margaret Laurence* that while Laurence didn't recall being influenced by any particular class, her literary training was part of her work's patterns and allusions, and her ability to critique her work and creative process with such precision and critical perception.

Laurence published in two student publications. One was the U. of M.'s paper, *The Manitoban*, which was distributed to the colleges. She said she mostly wrote poetry since she didn't have time to do prose, but fellow student Angela Graham said: "[W]e were all scribbling poetry." Graham recalled that while she didn't want anyone to read her own writing, Laurence said in the women's lounge one day that she couldn't wait to be published. Laurence also wrote in her memoir that she published her first poems in *The Manitoban* under the pseudonym Steven Lancaster, but that name didn't appear in any issues. There were, however, several poems under the bylines J.M.W., J.M. Wemyss, and finally different versions of her full name. Those started in mid-October 1944, weeks after she arrived at college, and ended in late 1946. Several were on war, the prairie, and loneliness, but two had religious images. "The Departure" included an interesting line—"Jesus, son of Joseph, I would have been your wife"—and another, "Clay-fettered Doors," had her turn from an altar to look in the streets "[f]or someone who answers to the name of God." In October 1946, she published one news report on a Columbia professor who spoke on tradition's role in society, but her contributions were more literary than journalistic.

Laurence's work was also published in United College's student magazine, the *Vox*, which was edited by her friend Jack Borland, though she became its assistant editor during her last three months at college. She published several poems in the spring of 1945, two of them for children: "Chants" was about sea caves and sunken treasures and "Cabbages" was about a butterfly living in a cabbage. Before she graduated in

May 1947, Laurence published several more poems and two stories in the *Vox*. "Calliope" was the story of carnival vendor German Joe's relationship with a runaway preschooler and "Tal des Walde" was a watchmaker's account of an Austrian count who established a feudal estate near Riding Mountain. She'd heard the count's story as a child, but later used it as the college story Morag wrote in *The Diviners*. The *Vox* also published Laurence's only critique, on the philosophy and early work of modern American poet Robinson Jeffers. Her interest in him earned her the 1947 yearbook comment that her mum had dropped a volume of Robinson Jeffers on her as a child and she'd been writing poetry ever since.

Laurence's college writing was capable, but it didn't foreshadow her later promise. It pointed to her dedication to writing and publishing, and earned many honours. She recalled getting a poetry prize and the highest English marks when she graduated in 1947, but United College later noted that she won several distinctions, including the Aikens Scholarship in Senior English.

United College's social gospel tradition was also critical to Laurence's development. The philosophy was ingrained in United's forerunner, Wesley College, when the Rev. Salem Bland, the Methodist minister who championed the movement, taught there in the early 1900s, but it was still promoted by many professors in the 1940s. John Graham, who studied ahead of Laurence and whose dad was United's principal, told me: "[W]e loved the idea of ensuring justice for all."

The social gospel was a liberal Protestant movement that professed that Christianity was just as concerned with changing the social and economic order as ensuring the faithful were personally saved. United Church historian Ian Manson explained that the social gospel's proponents saw Christ's life as the model for how people should live, and it took the Bible stories where Jesus challenged authority, included the outcasts, and cared for the poor, very seriously. They believed that the Holy Spirit was transforming people's consciousness so they would assume their share of collective responsibility for others. During the 1920s and 1930s, Canadian social gospellers urged governments to regulate big business, allow labour to bargain collectively, and allow conscientious objectors to avoid military service in the war. In the 1940s, some even criticized the government's role in interning Japanese Canadians. That was the kind of attitude prevalent at United College, which Laurence later noted, had "the kind of social conscience closely associated, in the prairies, with the Methodist and Presbyterian churches and, ultimately, with the United Church of Canada, in which I myself was brought up. From such a tradition had come many of the early reformers in the prairies, founders of the Social Democratic Party, the CCF, people such as J.S. Woodsworth, Stanley Knowles, Tommy Douglas, and many others."[6]

Social gospel discussions didn't end in class, either. They'd often continue after class or into the evening at Tony's, a coffee shop in the college basement. Almost everyone who attended United College recalled that the coffee shop was where students and professors gathered, and Laurence noted that their two favourite topics were religion and politics. Students, including theologs, discussed good and evil, whether God existed, why there were so many brands of Christianity, and other religions. They parsed society, social justice and injustice, ethical and moral attitudes toward society, and Russia's fight to survive. Laurence considered herself left wing, but John Graham said they all fancied themselves left wing then. It was the ethos, but it was also the kind of stimulating environment that Laurence would always gravitate to later in life whenever she had the chance.

CHAPTER 9

WAR LAYS A FOUNDATION

Laurence's social justice views began to sharpen in her college years, but never more than when real life intruded. It happened on vacation, but also when the atomic bombs were dropped on Japan, causing the war to climax in a way that forever altered her consciousness.

While Laurence was studying at home for her failed history course in July 1945, she took a vacation to visit Summerland, B.C., with her friend Madge. They picked cherries at "Paradise Ranch," where she wrote her college roommate, Helen (Warkentin) Stanley, that she loved the "friendly blue hills" and "pines that whispered at night." She didn't even mind rising at 4:45 a.m., but she was finally defeated by toting sixteen-foot ladders around the orchard. As she wrote Stanley: "It may have been God's country, but it certainly wasn't ours. So we left."

What Laurence liked were the people she met, who caused her to think. She told Stanley there were fruit farmers, girls from the wrong side of the tracks, immigrant women, high-school kids, and "returned men, with heaven knows what locked inside their minds—something that only showed in the occasional bitter twist of their mouths, or in their eyes, or in something they said cruelly." She added, "I think that they realize what the score is better than we do at college. They don't talk about their theories, they live them.... Don't get me wrong. I'm not turning against the college life or anything. But sometimes all the talking we do about theories of this & that seems rather futile & abstract. Not that I'm a highly practical creature—anything but—but it seems to me that the best in life comes from human relationships—friendship & love; & the understanding that comes of people working together, even if sometimes they don't particularly like each other. I think that a large part of what we get that's real & genuine we get from knowing people."[1]

Laurence was also touched when the war ended in 1945. She wrote Stanley on May 15 that it was wonderful that the European war was over, but she spent three days "feeling very sad about life in general." Three months later, when she was nineteen, the atomic bombs were dropped on Japan, ending the Asian-Pacific conflict. She wrote again that it was terrific that the Japanese surrendered, but she then foreshadowed the sentiments of her later activism when she said: "[T]he horrible thought keeps coming to me, & to prevent my utter jubilation, that it'll never be over in our lifetime, because of the effect it's had on all of our lives.... [O]n V night I actually felt sorry for the last generation, & somehow I wondered why they were celebrating. They've had their chance, & they've failed it—if people who try can ever fail. I kept thinking—it's our world now—the men & women of this generation, who are a little wiser and a little more clearsighted because of the war. I'm not talking about a brave new world or any eyewash like that. I don't think it'll be perfect—I don't even think it'll be a great deal better. But it's ours, to live in and have children and love and hate as we will.... [T]here is a certain sense of power in being able to live our own lives.... Anyway, these rather disjointed thoughts kept me awake all that night."[2]

United College's students discussed the end of the war when they returned to school that fall, and Laurence later reflected on their youthful belief that "[A] new and better and more just social order had to emerge. We would make sure that it did. The world could and would be a better place. Poverty could be eliminated. People could be in a free and peaceful world."[3] The students didn't realize the far-reaching effects of nuclear war, but they sensed the world would never be the same again. She said they also feared that the world could end: "We were the first generation in the whole world to know that humankind had the power to destroy itself, all other creatures, and the planet on which we lived."[4] It was a reality that would increasingly haunt her life as the implications emerged, and one to which she would eventually dedicate her passion.

Laurence was positioned for the future by the time she left college at twenty-one. As a young teen, she had felt called to write, and while at school, she met four mentors who encouraged it. She also started to shape her life's religious and socio-political themes, starting in high school and continuing in college. Those themes included the need to live in harmony with the earth, the importance of an individual's uniqueness, and her sense that people needed both God's grace and a strong sense of responsibility. She later said: "These basic tenets of my own social and religious faith were, I am sure, formed largely in my childhood and were added to and consolidated during my years at United College. Over the years, they have acquired more complexity."[5]

It was a foundation that was deeply rooted in her prairie background, but also the beginning of her spirit's journey. It would be a long and winding road, but she had a firm base that would help her keep going until she could finally share her passion with the world.

CHAPTER 10

MARRYING JACK LAURENCE

Peggy Wemyss was still a student when she met her husband, but she'd already had enough boy trouble to leave her disillusioned with the 1940s dating game and women's place in it.

The first man she fell in love with was Derek Armstrong, a British air force pilot whom she met in 1943, the summer she finished Grade 11 and turned seventeen. Their romance blossomed after the Royal Air Force (RAF) came to town, but ended with her desperately wanting to marry him, even years after he abandoned her.

The air school opened outside of Neepawa in 1941 and changed many young women's lives. The school was one of a series in western Canada that provided elementary flight training for the RAF's Commonwealth pilots, a new group of whom arrived every six weeks. The townsfolk tried to create a home away from home for the young men, and the teen girls had a role to play. Laurence's friend Mona (Spratt) Meredith said: "[We] were told to be patriotic. We had to dance with the boys, we had to entertain them. We were supposed to invite them out—for Sunday dinner or Easter dinner." Their hospitality often ended in more than that. Louise (Alguire) Kubik, one of Laurence's friends, met her first husband then and Laurence fell hard for Armstrong.

Armstrong was a handsome Brit who was a decade older than Laurence. She met him at one of the rowdy dances at Pedlar's, a converted garage where Neepawa's small band played its big band sound. She was thrilled that this well-read man who quoted poetry was interested in her. He took her to the base's classical musical evenings, introduced her to modern English poets, and even started exhibiting the attributes of a "classy liar," though she didn't realize it when he first told her that he was really the modern English composer Benjamin Britten. Her friends didn't like him because he broke dates with her, but Meredith said he, like Laurence, was more serious than the rest of them. The young couple would walk, dance, or visit at Laurence's place until her grandfather finally said the unpardonable—that Armstrong was probably married.

When Armstrong left town after his training, Laurence spent two years pining for news of him, wishing she'd married him. She finally got word through a mutual friend that he was still alive. She wrote her college roommate Helen (Warkentin) Stanley in June 1945: "[R]ight now I'd marry him tomorrow if it were possible, whether he explained or not."

The affair dissipated and she told several interviewers thirty years later that she had been desperately in love, but that she discovered a decade later that her grandfather was right: Armstrong was married.

Laurence was also disappointed by her college beau, Jack Borland, a war vet who arrived at United in 1945. They talked writing and literature and worked on the *Vox*. They also dated until late 1946, when he took another girl home from a party.

Once back on the dating scene, Laurence found it demeaning since girls were expected to play hard to get while boys seemed to prefer dumb females. She wrote in her memoir that even in college, the prettiest girls got dates and "you hoped and prayed that some guy, however gauche or bucktoothed, would ask you to one of the dances or to a film."[1] She obviously dated, though, because she was asked to leave residence in her last year after cavorting with a boy on the fire escape. She and her friend Mary (Turnbull) Mindess moved in together and lived in several places that year. One was a boarding house in Winnipeg's North End, a mile past the streetcar line. The boys who were to escort her to and from dates didn't usually have cars, so they floundered through snow, then necked on her porch at thirty below zero, and she said: "I rarely had a date with the same boy twice."[2] Her social life improved after they moved downtown, but then she ended up in a lovely rooming house on Roslyn Road, just south of the college. One day she spotted a man standing on the stairs: "I thought his face not only was handsome but also had qualities of understanding. I said to myself, 'That's the man I'd like to marry.'"[3]

That man was Jack Laurence, again ten years her senior. Laurence's biographer, Powers, said in *Alien Heart* that Jack lived in Alberta before he moved to England in 1936. He became an RAF sergeant and mechanic, then served in India during World War II, and taught in England before teaching at the air force base in Carberry, Manitoba. After he was discharged, Jack studied civil engineering at the U. of M. When he met Peggy, his mother was a writer who had published a novel and he was interested in writing and Third World development. Some of Laurence's friends said that he looked like Armstrong, and others had concerns about him as a life partner, but he was handsome and well travelled with a world view similar to hers. The couple was married in the Neepawa United Church on September 13, 1947. Laurence wrote in her memoir that they chose a church wedding as marriage was a commitment before God and a congregation, "a commitment made within a community to the future, to each other, and to life."[4]

CHAPTER 11

WINNIPEG'S NORTH END

The Laurences settled in Winnipeg's North End, which Laurence later said decided a lot of her life. She had her newspaper career there and met her best friend, Adele Wiseman. She also deepened her views and learned about another setting out of which she later tried to write.

Winnipeg's North End was where the city's immigrants settled in the early 1900s. It was an area immortalized in John Marlyn's novel, *Under the Ribs of Death*, and Adele Wiseman's first novel, *The Sacrifice*. By the 1940s, the North End held Ukrainian, Hungarian, Russian, Polish, German, and British immigrants with a mix of Protestant, Roman Catholic, Orthodox, Jewish, and militantly atheist viewpoints. They and their Canadian-born families were striving for a better life, often amidst poverty, poor housing, and prejudice. There were also many fiery politicians championing people's rights, creating a memorable milieu that appealed to Laurence.

The Laurences moved into the upper apartment of Anne and Bill Ross's duplex on Burrows Avenue. The Rosses were a fascinating couple in their mid-thirties. Bill had been a Communist since 1929. He'd been a school trustee, but was jailed during a strike and lived underground when the party was illegal. He served overseas in the army, and in 1948 became the provincial secretary of the Communist Party of Manitoba, then called the Labour-Progressive Party. Anne wasn't a Communist, but in 1948 became head nurse at the Mount Carmel Clinic in Winnipeg's inner city. The clinic had served the North End's Jewish immigrants, but was expanding to serve the wider community's needs, especially those of unwed mothers and young people at risk. Anne eventually became Mount Carmel's executive director and an ardent advocate on poverty and teen pregnancy issues. She and Laurence remained friends for life.

Laurence also became friends with Adele Wiseman in the North End. Wiseman recalled that they met in the summer of 1947 when they were both at the Ukrainian Labour Temple trying to get newspaper work. Wiseman was a feisty, inquisitive woman who was two years Laurence's junior, but they were both passionate about writing and the left-wing perspective. Wiseman's family lived across the street from the Rosses, so she recommended their apartment to Laurence. This started a lifelong friendship in which Wiseman published first and Laurence always remained a little deferential. It also soon made the Wisemans almost family to Laurence. Adele was the Canadian-born daughter of secularized Jews, Ukrainian immigrants who had struggled to survive the Depression. They were a financially poor tailor and dressmaker with four children, but they had a generosity, zest for life, and deep socialist sympathy that attracted Laurence. John Lennox, the York University English professor who edited two collections of Laurence's letters, told me their viewpoint further influenced her for "the Wisemans reinforced what was already there, but challenged her to grow politically." When Adele's mother, Chaika, died in 1980, Laurence said she'd been like a mother to her and a grandmother to her children.

As Laurence's contact grew with the Wisemans, it shrank with her own mum as their lives became more separate. Laurence still visited Neepawa occasionally, but her friend Meredith thought Margaret and Jack both didn't return as they didn't feel welcome. Laurence's mum was keen on her daughter's education, so she helped finance it by doing the hospital's accounting and secretarial work while the remaining family lived on very little. Mum finally sold the Big House because she thought it would be easier to cope with her dad's growing senility in their first, smaller home. Laurence later wrote: "I was too self-absorbed to want to look closely at what Mum went through when Grandfather, in his last years, would rant and rave, going out into the night streets of the town looking for his long-dead wife."[1] Laurence never lived in the Big House again and, once she left Winnipeg, she wrote her mum weekly, but only saw her four more times in the next eight years. Laurence was in Africa when her grandfather died at age ninety-six in 1953 and her mum moved to B.C. With the family gone, Laurence only returned to Neepawa twice more.

Winnipeg's North End fed Laurence's sympathies in many ways. When she had a residence named for her in Bethune College at Toronto's York University in 1983, she said she first learned about Dr. Norman Bethune in the North End when she met a couple of men from the Mackenzie-Papineau Battalion, the Canadians who fought against Franco and fascism in the Spanish Civil War. She told the crowd gathered for the occasion that those men described how Bethune died in China in 1939, "literally giving his own life, in the Chinese revolution, for what he believed in—social justice, and the healing of the torn and wounded, the suffering ordinary yet always extraordinary human beings who were determined to right the wrongs of countless centuries."[2] That was the kind of passionate dedication she admired and even tried to portray in her own way when she lived in the North End then. In 1948, she wrote a poem, "North Main Car—Winnipeg," which painted a word picture of the cosmopolitan area and the people on its streetcar. She noted those who'd come "from europe's handkerchief-sized farms, / from the winding streets of the world / exchanging the known devil, the overseer's whip, / for another, sight unseen." She also hinted at one of her future themes—"the past weaves the future on its loom." But she also referred to Winnipeg's great newspaper divide that she'd entered: "the ukrainian word and the canadian tribune? / or the ukrainian voice and the winnipeg free press. / two voices, two sides of the great ravine."[3] For those who knew the clues, it was obvious how political she had become.

CHAPTER 12

A NEWSPAPER CAREER

Laurence thought she would make her living as a writer by being a journalist, but she only worked on two newspapers and both were in Winnipeg. She started at *The Westerner* a few weeks before she married. It was a weekly Communist paper, which she didn't realize until after she began, but she was comfortable with it as she considered herself a Christian social democrat. As she later wrote: "Those old-time Communists in the forties in Winnipeg were not proposing violent revolution. They were proclaiming a need for social justice in terms of our land, and I discovered that many of their views were close to mine."[1] She only worked there for six months, but she learned a great deal as she did book reviews and a range of reporting, covering the social factors contributing to Winnipeg's polio epidemic and even the meat-packing workers' strike.

When *The Westerner* folded, she moved to the *Winnipeg Citizen*. It was born from a 1945 printers' strike against the *Winnipeg Free Press* and *Winnipeg Tribune*. The International

Typographical Union wanted the printers to get the same pay for fewer hours and it spread the strike across the Southam chain, trying to force a resolution in Winnipeg. Harry Ferns, a United College professor, wondered if people could use the opportunity to start a progressive newspaper more sympathetic to the city's unions and left-wing causes. He approached David Simkin, a North End Jewish printer he'd recently met, who then included Jock Brown, the general manager of a new farm machinery co-operative. They developed the prospectus for a small, left-wing, co-operatively owned newspaper and launched the organization in April 1946.

Laurence volunteered for the *Citizen* in that first summer of 1946 when students, striking printers, and sympathetic unionists were trying to raise funds for the new paper by selling five-dollar shares and fifty-dollar loan units. Mary (Turnbull) Mindess, Laurence's roommate who also knew Ferns from United College, tried to sell shares in Winnipeg's wealthy Tuxedo area while Laurence worked in the downtown organizing office. She had already done volunteer war work at the Central Volunteer Bureau in her first year of college, so she was experienced in phoning, typing, and filing. When we met at the Swayzes in 1978, she recalled being a lowly office worker in the *Citizen*'s organizing office, but she had fun stuffing envelopes and definitely believed in the cause. "I think most people came to the *Citizen* for the same reason I did," she said, "which was that we ... were extremely young and very idealistic and we liked the idea. We thought that Winnipeg needed another paper. We liked the idea of a co-operative newspaper in which the shareholders would have some influence on the policy. I think many of us hoped that the policies of the paper would be slightly more progressive than the policies of the *Tribune* or *Free Press*."

By the time Laurence returned to the *Citizen* after she married, its organizers had moved to the Simkins's North End print shop and were preparing to launch the paper. She hated office work but was a good typist, so she took a clerical job to get her foot in the door. When the *Citizen* began on March 1, 1948, she was one of its few, but eager reporters. She remembered it had some experienced newspaper men, "but an awful lot of us were enthusiastic youngsters who had to learn pretty quickly. There was a real sense of camaraderie because we were all so enthusiastic about the thing." Anne Ross later said: "She was very excited about the job. She used to come home full of marvellous stories and full of great crusading ideas of what she'd like to do, and what she would do if she were editor of the paper. And her eyes would sparkle.... Off she would go about the various things that she had experienced during the day and what she had written and what kind of stories she would really like to do.... [S]he was always talking about writing."[2]

Laurence couldn't remember how long she worked at the *Citizen*, but it appeared to be less than eight months. It was a busy time when she worked nights while Jack, who was finishing engineering, rose early to survey for the Prairie Farm Rehabilitation Administration. She wrote book reviews, news, and feature stories, and a simple daily, then weekly, radio column called "It's in the Air," which ran from March 1 until September 22, 1948. The day the paper began, though, she made up a feature story, "Café Mirrors Permanent; 'It's the Modern Touch,'" which ran on March 2, 1948. "The city editor asked me to do a feature article on mirrors in cafés and restaurants," she said. "You know, how do people react when they walk into a café. Do they look at themselves, avoid looking at themselves, you know, this kind of stuff. He wanted me to go into cafés and ask people. Well, I could cover the stories all right. But I was really, despite a somewhat brash manner, a shy young lady, and I thought to myself, 'I can't bring myself to go into cafés and restaurants and go around and ask a whole bunch of strangers how they felt about the mirrors.' So I simply sat down and made it all up." When I asked if it ran as the truth, she was startled: "Oh, sure. He thought it was a good story. I guess my talents for fiction were apparent even then.... I had been writing stories nearly all my life. So it wasn't very much of a trick to sit down and do it fictionally."[3] The printed story was an innocuous article that quoted a café owner, some clients, and waitresses on people who checked mirrors. Only her characteristic rapidly paced quotes might have given her secret away if anyone had recognized her style.

Laurence's main beat, however, was labour, which eventually led to the end of her *Citizen* career. She remembered being inexperienced: "[I]f it had not been for the kindness of some of those union men, I think I would have lost my job instantly because I knew so little about labour when I started." She covered union meetings, visited their offices, and wrote stories, but didn't realize there was a groundswell of anti-Communist feeling and a fear that the Communists could hijack the *Citizen*'s organization. The McCarthy era with all of its blacklists and recriminations was still to come, but that summer, the *Brandon Daily Sun* accused the *Citizen* of being Communist. While the *Sun* had to print a retraction, the *Citizen*'s managing editor, Bill Metcalfe, who came from the *Free Press* and CBC, was worried that the Communists would take over the paper's co-op board just when it was struggling financially. Communist leader Bill Ross later said the *Citizen*'s organizers initially asked the Communist Party for support, but then the newspaper's staff distanced themselves from it.[4] But Metcalfe said he had to take seriously the allegation that one of his staff was a Communist.[5]

Metcalfe eventually confirmed that Laurence was the reporter. He said she was a very good reporter, but he "eventually got a very strong complaint against this person from the Trades and Labour Council," which wasn't right wing. "They said, 'Look, we don't want any part of that person again covering our meetings. That person is a Communist.'" When I asked Laurence, she told me what a staff member had said: "[T]hey were very unhappy because, after having been warned, I still continued to have lunch from time to time at a café across the street with a couple of friends of mine who were Communist." She noted that she'd always considered herself "quite left wing": "There were a number of young people who had been students ... who were not at first actively involved but were really in a sense members of the 'old left.' We used to sit around and discuss how we were going to save the world." She was also still living with the Rosses, who were close friends, so she added: "Nobody was accusing me of anything, but it was a rather tense atmosphere." The rumours spread about her fate, so she said: "Great, if they're thinking of firing me, I quit, as of now." Metcalfe confirmed it: "While I was debating what I was going to do, she up and quit."

Laurence left the *Citizen* sometime after her September 29 column, but well before the paper went into receivership on April 13, 1949. She remembered working at the Bay's book department for a few weeks before Christmas, then one of Jack's friends helped her find work as the YWCA's registrar. She loved that job with "all the little kids running in and out of the office all the time." But, she decided not to pursue journalism any further since fiction and reporting were "two different types of professions": "[I]f I really wanted to write fiction then the kind of job I should get would be a nine to five office job that took as little of the mental processes as possible." Her reporting experience still taught her to be concise, not to show off with big words, and how to organize her thoughts and material. "So I think it was valuable in a sense," she told me. "I wouldn't have wanted to go on working in journalism." Once at the Y, though, she began writing evenings and weekends again: "I had a lot more both time and mental energy."[6]

CHAPTER 13

GLOBE-TROTTING

Jack graduated from the University of Manitoba's School of Engineering in the spring of 1949 and the Laurences left for England. Peg, as she now called herself, had only been out of Manitoba a few times before, so looked forward to her journey abroad, though she didn't know then that what she found would only point her back home again.

When the Laurences arrived in England in July 1949, London was still recovering from the war, but the young couple liked the socially progressive Labour government, which was so different from Canada's reigning Liberals. Jack was hired by an engineering firm while Peg worked for a small employment agency that sometimes challenged her by then well-honed progressive sensibilities. As she wrote in her diary then: "I see a lot of rich-bitches, who can't run a house without six servants, and who tell you that they won't hire 'foreigners.'"[1]

Money was tight, so the Laurences rented a Hampstead bed-sitter. They visited Paris after winning $250 in a football pool and attended films, theatre, and concerts as often as they could. But Peg's leftist sympathies were never far from the surface. After hearing Beethoven's *Ninth*, she wrote her friend Adele Wiseman that he was a revolutionary because he included Friedrich Schiller's brotherhood of man theme from *Ode to Joy*. Given that she'd been in Winnipeg when the *Citizen* failed to raise enough money at a public forum to continue, she added: "My advice to a progressive rally would be to invest in a really good orchestra, conductor and massed choir; perform Beethoven's Ninth, with the Ode to Joy being sung in English; then take up the collection immediately afterwards! The result would be stupendous!"[2]

Laurence's writing continued to develop a progressive edge in this time. The *Canadian Tribune*, the Communist Party of Canada's paper, published her first poem after college in January 1950. She wrote Wiseman, with whom she carried on a lifelong correspondence: "I was, and am, tremendously pleased and encouraged." While she said her poem wasn't great, it also wasn't a propaganda poem, which "is one where the propaganda matters more than the poem."[3] She'd sent the *Tribune* a better poem about the recent Italian peasants' revolt, but there is no record of it being published since it was not bylined. But even the novel she started then had a message. It was about a young, small-town woman who fell in love with a Ukrainian boy she met at college and then had to deal with her and her family's prejudice against his background. That was the first time in which her Neepawa sensitivities obviously surfaced, but it also picked up on some of the small-town prejudice that would later lace her second Canadian novel, *A Jest of God*.

Laurence found Wiseman a part-time job in London just before she and Jack left for Africa in December 1950. Wiseman, who'd been doing odd jobs for a year while writing her first novel, *The Sacrifice*, arrived in August 1950 to work at the Stepney Jewish Girls' Club. The two friends barely had time to read each others' work before the Laurences left. Jack was tired of his office job and wanted outdoor work that needed doing—not, as Laurence later wrote in *The Prophet's Camel Bell*, paving a gravel road, but building one. He'd applied to the British Colonial Office in June after seeing its ad for the British Protectorate of Somaliland. Somaliland had been strategically important to the British, French, and Italians since the Suez Canal opened in 1869. By 1950, Somaliland had three sections—British, French, and United Nations—and the Colonial Office wanted a civil engineer to build thirty earth dams along a waterless three-hundred-mile area north of the Ethiopian border. The dams would hold rainwater so the nomadic Somalis, which was most of the population, could graze their flocks in the dry season. Jack was offered the job, but the Colonial Office said Peg couldn't go for at least six months as there was no married couples housing. Jack carefully explained that his hardy Canadian wife was used to living in a tent, even though she'd never camped before. "[F]ortunately," she later wrote in *The Prophet's Camel Bell*, "the Colonial Office was convinced by the striking description Jack gave of me as an accomplished woodswoman, a kind of female Daniel Boone, and I was permitted to go."

The Laurences arrived in Somaliland in January 1951 and spent six years in Africa, their time framed by Jack's jobs and their children's births. They lived in East Africa's Somaliland from January 1951 until June 1952, then left after Jack felt he'd learned all that he could from building the first dams. Jocelyn was born on their leave in London in August 1952, then they moved to West Africa's Gold Coast, where they stayed until 1957, just before it became the Republic of Ghana. This time, Jack was one of the British Public Works' top men on a project to turn the fishing village of Tema, thirty-two kilometres east of the capital of Accra, into a port that would serve the eastern Gold Coast. He also directed construction of a road between Accra and Tema, and they lived first outside of Accra and then in Tema. David was born in Accra in August 1955, and Laurence's family was complete by the time she was twenty-nine. That was important to her since she'd grown up believing that she had to have her children before she was thirty. She really wanted a family, but had learned the hard way that she tended to miscarry, just like her birth mother, Verna, who miscarried twice before giving birth to her.

Laurence's reaction to Africa was as mixed as her reaction to her hometown of Neepawa. She loved the Somali people and customs, but especially the land, and wrote Wiseman soon after arriving: "[T]he land is empty; the sky is open from one side of the horizon to the other." She later said its desert was "a kind of country I took to right away because, as in the prairies, you can see from one side of the horizon to the other.... [T]he kind of country I like best has that sense of openness."[4] The Gold Coast was more lush and humid with a strong British and Christian influence, but there were Muslims, and the African religious and tribal ways were prevalent in the interior. Its nationalism was strong and she liked the fact that Prime Minister Kwame Nkrumah was moving it toward independence. It was also a plus that many of the educated people preferred to blend African tribal culture with modern ways rather than simply imitate the European way.

Having been raised in Canada, a former British colony, Laurence struggled with Africa's colonial rulers. She said she grew up reading books "that told us the British Empire was the best thing in the world," so she was already "vigorously anti-colonialist."[5] She later added that Canada was a country which many people believed still to be suffering from a colonial outlook. "Like most Canadians I took umbrage swiftly at a certain type of English who felt they had a divinely bestowed superiority over the lesser breeds."[6] The few English she'd known in Neepawa tended to be remittance men's families, so by the time she reached Africa, she particularly detested anyone like "the 'remittance men', languid younger sons of county families, men who could not have fixed a car nor driven a tractor to save their souls and who looked with gentlemanly amusement on those who could, men who had believed they were coming to the northern wilds and who in our prairie and mountain towns never once found occasion to change their minds."[7]

Given her background and sentiments, Laurence grew increasingly uncomfortable with Africa's colonial trappings and some of the colonizers' attitudes. She protested when Jack hired a houseboy, Mohamed, and hated being called Memsahib in Somaliland (and Madam in Ghana), which was, she wrote, "a word which seemed to have connotations of white man's burden, paternalism, everything I did not believe in."[8] She was shocked when someone called the police, who tailed Mohamed and her through Hargeisa's market soon after she arrived because European women didn't do that. She was repulsed by the European women's tea parties—much as she had been by her mum's tea parties in Neepawa and the college sororities in Winnipeg. She especially detested the denigrating advice that these women gave about their servants. Her feelings were such that she didn't even like visiting the few pleasant European women when she was pregnant and living alone in Hargeisa, even though her only other companion was Mohamed, a member of an outcast tribe who tried to sell her things, and a few Somali girls for whom Mohamed had to translate since she didn't know enough Somali. The result was that by the time she left Somaliland, she'd grown to loathe its racist colonizers. As she later wrote in *The Prophet's Camel Bell*: "Every last one of these people purported to hate Africa, and yet they all clung to an exile that was infinitely preferable to its alternative— nonentity in England. I have never in my life felt such antipathy towards people anywhere as I felt towards these pompous or whining sahibs and memsahibs."[9]

Laurence's anti-colonialist reaction escalated on the Gold Coast, where she made few friends. She tried unsuccessfully to impress the Africans that she met there by telling them she appreciated their culture and move toward independence, but she later said: "It's extraordinarily difficult to form a close friendship with somebody of a totally different culture because there is a great deal of misunderstanding ... even if you're speaking the same language, you're speaking out of a different conceptual background."[10] The Laurences lived in Jack's company complex with its European employees, but she said she still wore her "militant liberalism like a heart on my sleeve,"[11] so she was quick to point out to those who didn't believe independence was imminent that their "years of privilege and arrogance were swiftly coming to an end." She was so vehement: "There were times when old colonials walked out of a cocktail party on account of remarks I had made. I *was* tactless. I was tactless, though, because I believed profoundly in what I was saying."[12]

Laurence's views had grown increasingly strident since Winnipeg, but she later said it was Africa that really taught her to look at herself. She found "just having the heart in the right place is not enough."[13] She decided that the best thing the colonialists could do was to leave and let Africans solve their own problems, but said: "What I learned, and this comes out in *The Prophet's Camel Bell*, was that the small *l* liberal can, without meaning to, be incredibly condescending."[14] It was an attitude she'd worked to unleash from her staunch prairie Presbyterianism while at college, but then spent two decades trying to guard against so she would not offend those she appreciated.

CHAPTER 14

WRITING IN AFRICA

While Jack's work in Africa was obvious, Peg's was not. She wanted to get to know the Somali country and people, so—unlike most European women—she often joined Jack and his crew in their desert camp. It was a hard life. The tribesmen initially didn't trust Jack and challenged him. The Laurences were caught in a rain storm that threatened to destroy their camp, a desert flood that almost swept them away, and a blinding sand storm that hampered their attempt to deliver equipment. Peg initially found a place by nursing, which recalled her Neepawa plan to become a nurse before she was called to be a writer. She'd doctor the camp crew with her first aid kit, and her reputation as a healer quickly spread after she cured one man's earache with Dettol-laced water. But at one point, she hid her kit because she couldn't do enough for the Somalis starting to arrive at the camp with everything from an infected camel bite to dehydration. She felt particularly helpless before the women who wanted assistance for their children dying of malaria, or relief from their own pain from menstruation or intercourse following their clitorectomies. That augmented her growing awareness of the women's hard lives in the desert and stirred Laurence's sensitivity to the plight of other women and their families, a concern that would grow over the years.

Laurence's own community in Somalia finally began to centre around her new writing project. She was still working on her novel and teaching some of Jack's staff English when she had the idea to translate Somali poems to show the English that the Somalis had poetry. Gus Andrezejewski, a Polish scholar and poet studying Somali, encouraged her, so she started reading the Koran and learning Somali, which, she wrote Wiseman, was a "hellish language."[1] The Somalis didn't initially support her work, but she eventually convinced Gus's assistant, the Somali poet Musa Haji Ismail Galaal, that the project had merit, and the two men translated for her. Her language teacher, Hersi Jama, also told her stories and gathered others from tribal elders and storytellers, but screened what he told a European woman. Her circle widened to include others who helped, and she worked hard to craft an equivalent English poem or story. She eventually collected thirty poems and thirty-six tales in *A Tree for Poverty*, and then had some luck getting it published.

Laurence was in danger of miscarrying when she was pregnant with Jocelyn, so moved to the city of Hargeisa. She lived alone weekdays, but got lonely writing and became secretary to Philip Shirley, the chief administrator of the British Protectorate of Somaliland Secretariat. At first, she thought he was a cold, dispassionate imperialist, but he read her manuscript and decided the government should publish it. By then, she'd decided that the project was important to preserve the Somalis' oral folk literature, which could be lost in fifty years without a common written language. While doing the work, she identified ten types of poetry and some moral contrasts in the stories that resembled those in the Bible and English literature, but she later wrote that Shirley pointed to a description of the Somali tribesmen's precarious life in the dry season and said: "It would be worth while for this one passage in your introduction."[2] When she moved to the Gold Coast in 1952, she left the manuscript with Shirley. He finally got a grant to publish it in Kenya in 1954 and sent her a published copy.

A Tree for Poverty was an amazing accomplishment for a woman of twenty-six and the Peace Corps later used it to orient volunteers to Somalia. But she was critical of it when she wrote the preface to the second edition that McMaster University Library Press published in 1970. She still believed that her collection was important since it was the first English translation and conveyed some of the nomads' sense of life, but she dismissed all of the accolades that the Somalis and scholars bestowed on her for understanding the Somalis and their literature. She even called her translations amateurish and her introduction condescending in the way of white liberals. It was still good enough to steal, though. After reading Danish writer Izak Dinesen's *Shadows on the Grass* in 1961, Laurence discovered that, in 1959, the Dane John Buccholzer had plagiarized her work in his book *The Horn of Africa: Travels in British Somaliland.* She angrily contacted his publisher, asking that the matter be addressed, but the wrong was never corrected.

Laurence kept writing, but had more fiction attempts than successes in those years. She kept diaries in Somaliland so she could write a book about it later. In Ghana, she continued to do Somali translations for Andrezejewski and wrote scripts on Africa for the CBC. In late 1951, she finally abandoned the novel that she'd started. She'd tried to fit everything she knew in it, and told Wiseman it ended up too long with "too many people, too many themes ... the thing doesn't hold together properly."[3] She finally quit, saying: "[I]t stinks. It really wasn't what I wanted at all."[4]

Her Somali stories were working and she finished four by November 1951. Even before they were done, she wrote: "Listen, Adele, they're good!... I think ... they're the only good things I've ever written in prose, except for odd passages here and there." The difference was, she continued: "[F]or the first time in my life I really tried to write as I thought my characters would think, and not as I thought myself." The stories were written mostly as conversation, not "propaganda," and she discovered as she reread her novel that she grew pompous when she went much beyond conversation. She added: "I seem to do better sticking to what people actually say, and letting the reactions and feelings and any deeper significance show up between the lines."[5]

Laurence started sending her stories to publications, but most of them were rejected until 1953. Whit Burnett, *Story*'s editor in New York, published "Uncertain Flowering" in late 1953. It was a story about an English teen who spent her holidays with her parents, part of Somaliland's British elite, and tried to bed their friend after he confirmed her parents' infidelity. When Burnett contacted her about publishing it, he also asked if she had a novel. By then, she doubted that she could write one, but she started again, and by mid-1953, had one hundred pages of a Somali novel seen from a European woman's perspective. She restarted it that fall when it bogged down. In the meantime, Malcolm Ross, her former professor who edited *Queen's Quarterly*, also asked for some stories or translations and rejected one of each before accepting a story which she finally replaced with a new Ghana story, "The Drummer of All the World," which was published in the Winter 1956 edition. It was a powerful tale of an English missionary's son who grew up in Ghana but returned after independence to discover the distance between him and his former African friends. Walter Swayze, a professor who had met Laurence at United College in 1946, said: "It was so much better than anything I'd seen before it almost took my breath away."[6]

The Laurences went on leave in England in late 1955, and when Peg returned, she started what she thought was a story, but soon discovered was a new novel. Ever since she had had children, she'd struggled to find time to write. By then, she was doing all of the domestic work, so when the story started flowing, she wrote after Jack went to bed at ten-thirty and worked until two or three in the morning four nights a week. She later said: "I scribbled on and on, as though a voice were telling me what to write down. It was the easiest novel I ever wrote because I knew absolutely nothing about writing a novel. The pages poured out."[7] She finally laid out the various episodes on her dining room table and found there was no structure. She found their connecting points, cut, and began alternating English and African chapters, but was still discouraged by the time she turned thirty in July 1956. Wiseman was about to publish her first novel, *The Sacrifice*, which would win the Governor General's Award, but Peg was still working on her third attempt at a novel and feeling beaten up by her gruelling schedule. She finally finished the draft of *This Side Jordan* before leaving Africa in 1957 and returned to Vancouver, where she sought her dying mum's help one last time.

CHAPTER 15

LIFE IN VANCOUVER

The Laurences were already planning to return to Canada for their children's education in 1957 when they received a telegram in late 1956 that Peg's mum, Marg Wemyss, was dying of cancer. Peg and the kids left in January 1957, and Jack followed that spring. Peg visited her friends, Wiseman in London and Meredith in Vancouver, then flew to Victoria, where her mum had lived with her sister, Ruby, ever since their dad had died in Neepawa four years earlier.

Peg had only seen her mum four times in the eight years since she left Canada. The Laurences brought Marg to London before Jocelyn was born and again for David's christening. They also visited her in Canada in 1954, when Peg thought her mum looked old and tired from the hard life she'd lived with her dad, Grandfather Simpson. The last time Laurence saw her mum in London in 1955, she gave her a long letter as Marg left. Laurence later wrote: "I had no premonitions. I simply wanted to tell her (and for me, this was more possible on the page than in speech) how much I loved her, how much she meant to me, and how much her encouragement of my writing had strengthened me, even though I had had nothing published professionally. I also wanted to tell her that she could not have been more my mother if she had actually borne me."[1]

Marg was home from the hospital when Peg arrived, but she was weak and on painkillers. Peg moved in with her mum and aunt, and Laurence said: "The next three months were among the most difficult and anguished of my life."[2] Not only did she have two preschoolers to keep busy as her mum died, but the five of them were squeezed in a small house and Peg needed her privacy. She finally built a make-shift bedroom of clothesline and blankets next to her kids' room in the basement and created a desk out of a door on two trunks so she could keep working late on her novel. She grew as fond of that space as her old Neepawa playhouse, and it helped her cope.

Peg and her mum never discussed Marg's impending death, but Laurence eventually showed her the novel's second draft. Marg found it hard to concentrate, but spent three hours reviewing it, just as she used to review Peg's writing in Neepawa. Laurence said: "We were back, suddenly, to her critic-teacher, lover-of-literature self, and I, to my young self. It was her final gift to me. It was as though the illness, for some hours, fell away. She analyzed my novel with the same perception and fairness, the same hard, reliable honesty she had always had."[3] Marg told Laurence that she'd written a moving portrayal of the West Africans torn between the worlds of their ancestors and Western education, hating colonialism and wanting independence, but stereotyped the whites. Laurence heard that criticism again before the novel was published, but told her mum the book was dedicated to her. Marg didn't live long enough to see it published.

Marg Wemyss, at about age sixty-seven, died of pancreatic cancer in September 1957. Peg visited her mum twice after the Laurences moved to Vancouver. She stayed three weeks the last time and visited the hospital daily with her brother Bob, who lived in Nanaimo. Peg wrote to Wiseman after Marg's death: "[T]hat was the most ghastly period I've ever lived through."[4] Marg weakened, needed morphine, then became irrational, and all that she remembered from the present were her children's names before she slid into a coma. Bob and Peg weren't there when Marg died, but Laurence said neither she nor her mum liked people seeing them off on trips. Marg's hard, slow death would impact Laurence's own choices at the end of her life, and she wrote in her memoir: "I have the feeling that, when I die, I won't need my children to be there at the last moment."[5]

Once in Vancouver, Laurence's life evolved into a routine similar to the one she had in Africa, but she was stressed trying to juggle it all. Jack found an engineering job while she marked engineers' English papers for the University of British

Columbia, and after publishing her first story in *Prism*, she wrote book reviews for the *Vancouver Sun*. She kept writing fiction, working at nights until David was in school, then fitting it around her housework during the day. She occasionally had to pare back, but constantly felt torn trying to be wife, mother, and writer. Her letters noted the drain of it all while her biographers said she was often angry and impatient with her family. She later noted: "My sense of being torn apart, in those five years in Vancouver, was severe. It reached its peak when my first novel was published in 1960."[6] Even after that success, she felt her writing was "stolen time" and she could never quite achieve the "hoped-for balance."[7] She wished she could get a Canada Council grant to hire a cleaning woman, and vowed not to work so late, but then she couldn't help it when another novel was being born. She later noted: "When the writing was demanding to be put down on the page, it was difficult to have to leave it in order to make meals, look after the kids, and try to be a sympathetic and loving wife. There were times when I didn't succeed and felt like I was attempting an impossible juggling act."[8]

The Laurences weren't happy in Vancouver. Jack switched jobs, but didn't feel he was doing all that he could and wanted to work overseas. They considered it in 1960, but Margaret— as she called herself after her first novel was published—was concerned about the children's education. The Laurences had a few friends, but the relationships weren't always easy. Her

Neepawa pals, Meredith and Kubik, and their spouses were there, but the couples didn't always get along. Many in Neepawa believed Margaret was a Communist, especially after her *Citizen* experience, and Kubik's first husband thought both Laurences were Communist. He wasn't always polite, and dinner parties often ended with Margaret being angry. She didn't find the camaraderie she desired in Vancouver's writing community, either. She left one party feeling utterly hopeless after a discussion on the purpose of art because she felt most of the writers' talk was so abstract that it was "phoney baloney." She also felt her writing didn't fit. As she wrote Wiseman: "I can only do one thing—I can tell stories.... This is not, and never will be, first-rate stuff, but for what it is, it is honest, and my talking pretentiously about art is not going to make it first-rate stuff."9

Ethel Wilson was the one beacon Laurence found in Vancouver. Wilson was then seventy-three and one of Canada's best writers, and she and Laurence had much in common as Wilson had been born in Africa, orphaned, and lived in England. Despite being married to a prominent doctor, Wilson was also as sympathetic to labour and the social gospel as Laurence.

The two women met after Wilson wrote Laurence to praise the first story she published in *Prism*, "The Merchant of Heaven." When Laurence replied, Wilson invited her for tea in January 1961. Laurence later wrote: "That meant more to me than I can ever express and began a friendship which has been one of the most valued in my life."[10] She found Wilson to be a wise, gracious lady who provided her with "[t]he sense that somebody did understand. There's no question that I would have gone on writing, but she provided me with an enormous amount of encouragement."[11] Wilson, meanwhile, found Laurence to be talented and unaffected, and hoped that she had a future as a writer.[12] The two often met to discuss books and writers, and Wilson continued to encourage Laurence's writing even after she moved to England, while Laurence remained in touch after Wilson moved to a nursing home. When Wilson died in January 1981, Laurence wrote a tribute in the *Toronto Star*, noting how important Wilson's friendship was: "I was starved for the company of other writers, and here was an older woman whose work I admired so much taking the time to talk with and encourage a young and unknown writer."[13] Laurence also told *NeWest Review*: "I owe her a great, great deal. There's no way that I can ever repay her personally.... The only thing I can do is pass it on."[14] It was a legacy that built on the support Laurence received on the prairies, but it also became part of her legacy, as one of the things that Laurence is still most remembered for is how much she supported younger writers.

CHAPTER 16

WRITING FROM AFRICA TO CANADA

Laurence's Vancouver years were personally strained, but professionally productive. She wrote most of her African work and started her Canadian fiction. Despite her fear that the change would end her career since she wasn't writing about Africa, it was pivotal to moving it forward.

Laurence finished *This Side Jordan* in 1957, and her mother-in-law, Elsie Fry Laurence, a writer, convinced her to enter it in *Atlantic Monthly's* novel contest.[1] The *Atlantic's* editor rejected it, but said that he would reconsider it if she rewrote the European parts. She did, but the *Atlantic* rejected it again as it already had several African novels. She finally got a break in 1959 when the UBC professor for whom she was marking, Gordon Elliott, asked Jack McClelland to read her manuscript. McClelland said he'd publish it if he could find an American publisher. She suggested Macmillan & Co. in Britain, then St. Martin's Press in New York agreed, and the novel was released in 1960. Within a year, her career started to take shape as McClelland persuaded an American agent to represent her, and she won the Canadian Authors' Association's Beta Sigma Phi award for a first novel.

This Side Jordan was Laurence's first book about freedom. It was set in Ghana during its transition from colonialism to independence. The novel was centred around two key characters—Nathaniel, an African teacher, who lost his traditional way of life without firmly grasping the new way that was emerging, and Miranda, the inquisitive wife of a British accountant, who tried to befriend Nathaniel but found that her white liberalism patronized him. The novel was rich in detail and social conscience, portraying the lives of both the British and Africans caught in the transition. But Laurence later said that the alternating English and African chapters didn't work, and despite her mum's and publisher's criticism that the European chapters were weaker, she thought those were her best: "In the end, I was able to understand the Europeans best, I think, even though my sympathy with colonial Europeans was certainly minimal or even non-existent."[2]

This Side Jordan was interesting because Laurence always said that her writing wasn't autobiographical, but the book echoed her African sentiments and experience. It reflected her anti-colonialism and she later said that it showed her why Africans didn't like white liberals. Miranda also seemed a lot like her since she was young and full of faith then, but she also empathized with the Africans, who treated her with polite tolerance. Biographer James King said the Laurences met a teacher, Ofosu, in 1952, who was the model for Nathaniel. She described their relationship in "The Very Best Intentions," an essay she wrote in 1964, though she called him Mensah in it. Their cultural clash—where his protective stonewalling met her liberal sympathy—and even the fact that their sons were born at the same time in the same hospital were reflected in the novel.

While Laurence was trying to get *This Side Jordan* published, she wrote a series of stories set in Ghana, which were collected in *The Tomorrow-Tamer* in 1963. They appeared from 1959 to 1963 in *Prism*, *Saturday Evening Post*, *The Tamarack Review*, and *Winter's Tales*. Canadian critic George Woodcock said that her first stories made Canadians aware there was an important, new voice among them. The stories showed the British and Africans' lives, and many contained poignant details about African villages. Laurence won the University of Western Ontario's President's Medal for two of them in 1961 and 1962, but the stories had the same problem as *This Side Jordan*: her anti-colonial message was so strong that it often distracted from the story. Woodcock said the main flaw was "the obviously didactic intent, for in almost every story there is a moral which the author has not sufficiently absorbed into the fabric of the action."[3]

After writing *This Side Jordan*, Laurence read French psychologist Dominique Mannoni's *Prospero and Caliban: The Psychology of Colonization*. She said: "[I]t struck me with the force of revelation"[4] because he drew the same conclusions about colonialism that she'd drawn from her African experience and writing. They both felt that the British in Africa, especially those who were condescending and brutal to the Africans, left their culture because they lacked a certain human quality, and they also couldn't compete with their peers. She said she wrote her best story, "The Voices of Adamo," after reading Mannoni, but Clara Thomas noted that Mannoni's influence reached "into all of her writing, for its theme is her theme of exile and its pages both suggest and confirm the emotional situations and their psychological bases which she has worked out in the lives of her characters."[5] Walter Swayze told me he always felt that "Margaret had already learned what Mannoni said, but her reading of him gave her confidence because of the way he had formulated it and because he was such a 'hot property' when it came out."

Laurence's career was finally starting, but she'd reached a crossroads. She wanted to finish her African stories and publish a collection, but McClelland insisted that it wouldn't sell until she wrote another novel. She resurrected the Somali novel she'd abandoned in Africa, but found it superficial. By January 1961, she was tired of Africa and said she wanted to write something about Somaliland from her diaries, then "put paid to that phase of my life. It's over, and I have a strange sense of release and relief." She abandoned the novel, but was drawn to writing about her own country, which coincided with her mental state. As she wrote Wiseman: "I feel I'm here to stay, for better or worse, and that I don't need to go away any more, in fact can't go away. It's here, and in me, and I can't run forever to countries (real or imaginary) which I like because they didn't know me when I was young." While she said she'd hated Canada for most of her life, she was beginning to see why: "It's the mirror in which one's own face appears, and like Queen Elizabeth the First, you smash the mirrors but that doesn't change yourself after all." For the first time, she said, "I feel the urge to write about the only people I can possibly know about from the inside."[6]

That desire led her back to an old woman's story that she'd been mulling over since her mum was dying in 1957. Laurence had become increasingly interested in old age and the ways that people meet it, but it took awhile to summon the courage to start *The Stone Angel*. When she finally did in late 1961, she didn't think anyone would like it, but told Wiseman she'd already abandoned two novels that were "dead as doornails. Then this daft old lady came along, and I will say about her that she is one hell of an old lady, a real tartar. She's crabby, snobbish, difficult, proud as lucifer for no reason, a trial to her family, etc. She's also—I forgot to mention—dying. The outcome is known from the first page. The whole thing is nuts—I should have my head examined. Who wants to read about an old lady who is *not* the common public concept of what an old lady should be? Obviously no one. Sometimes I feel so depressed about this, I think I will take up ceramics or something soothing. But I can't help it, Adele. I have to go on and write it."[7]

Laurence later said *The Stone Angel* wrote itself more easily than anything she ever did, but it also presented challenges as she finally faced her past. Writing the first draft, she explained, "was a wonderful release. To my amazement, idiomatic expressions I hadn't thought about for years came back to me, as did visual memories of the town and the valley and the hill. Manawaka is not Neepawa, but many of the descriptions of places, the houses, the cemetery on the hill, are based on my memory of the town that was my world when I was learning the sight of my own eyes. The novel poured forth. It was as if the old woman was actually there, telling me her life story, and it was my responsibility to put it down as faithfully as I could."[8] Unlike her African characters, Laurence was sure of Hagar, who spoke in the voice of her grandparents' generation. She noted: "[F]or the first time since I had become a professional writer, I knew that I was getting it just right."[9] But she struggled with the prairie pioneers, who were "pig-headed old egotists who can't relinquish the reins," then she struggled with herself. As she wrote Wiseman: "This whole novel is something that goes so far back, with me, and is such a wrenching up of my background that it is difficult for me to be honest enough."[10] She was also afraid that some people would be offended since they wouldn't realize characters are "given to you—and that they are not copied from individual persons."[11] The irony was that she later said Hagar was part of her Scots prairie background, but she also told her friend Budge Wilson that Grandfather Simpson was the model.

Laurence revised and typed the draft, then wrote to Wiseman in August 1962 that she'd abandoned it because it was too boring. Depressed, she said: "I wonder if I can write anything about this country. I can see now why I found it easier to write stories etc set in Africa—it is a kind of screen, an evasion, so that one need never make oneself vulnerable. Also, when I write about people here, my old inhibitions come up all over again. Maybe I could do something with stories set here if I weren't living here."[12] She later said that she was scared because the novel meant so much to her: "I thought if it was rejected by a publisher, it would be more than I could bear."[13]

After Laurence set *The Stone Angel* aside in 1961, she returned to her Somaliland diaries and wrote *The Prophet's Camel Bell*. She wasn't sure anyone would care about the experiences she and Jack had had a decade earlier, but she was glad she hadn't tackled the book earlier as it would have been filled with pompous theories about colonial administration, and now she just wanted to tell what had happened. Clara Thomas said it was the hardest book that Laurence ever wrote because she used the diaries as reference, recreated situations, then tried to understand them from a decade's distance. The result was a fascinating blend of biography and portrait—of the Laurences and the people they met. Laurence began by saying that when she left for Africa, the last thing she expected was "that the strangest glimpses you may have of any creature in the distant lands will be those you catch of yourself."[14] She then showed some of her personal growth, but also drew portraits of the British colonizers, men in Jack's camp, a child prostitute who followed their camp, and nomads dying from drought and malaria. By the time she finished the book, though, she seemed more like an observer in Jack's world than a participant in her own. She wrote Wiseman that it was her farewell to Somaliland, but she noted in her memoir that it was "dedicated to Jack, for it was our common story. I think I half-realized that it was almost my farewell to him."[15]

The Prophet's Camel Bell was published in 1963 in England and Canada, and in 1964 in the U.S., but as soon as it was accepted in 1962, she discounted it as "too nice."[16] She later said that she never felt her non-fiction books counted because "they're not true enough, not penetrating enough, or at least they don't speak as much of my own truth as I have sometimes been able to speak in novels."[17] In 1962, she wrote Gordon Elliott, the Vancouver friend for whom she'd marked papers that she'd tried to be honest, but "I have felt this way for a long time, that my writing has come to have something false in it.... I have been undergoing a kind of intensive soul-searching lately ... and perhaps something will come of it—we will see. I am beginning to see, I think, what I have to do. My mother told me long ago—'some people think it is better to write about what you know,' but I guess it has taken me some time to find out that she was right."[18]

Laurence later reflected on this transitional era with a quiet dispassion. She said her African books were "written by an outsider who experienced a seven years' love affair with a continent but who in the end had to remain in precisely that relationship, for it could never become the close involvement of family."[19] She then added: "I was fortunate in going to Africa when I did—in my early twenties—because for some years I was so fascinated by the African scene that I was prevented from writing an autobiographical first novel."[20] She also knew that writing that type of first novel would have been wrong for her: "[M]y view of the prairie town from which I had come was still too prejudiced and distorted by closeness. I had to get farther away from it before I could begin to see it."[21] That distance was already occurring, and the woman and her writing that most people now remember was beginning to emerge.

CHAPTER 17

LIFE AT THE CROSSROADS

Laurence's years in Vancouver, and the launch of her career, changed more than her writing. By the time she left Canada again, her life and its impact on her work was shifting, too.

One of the first shifts was the increasing impact that the spiritual had on her life and work. That influence had been there since her teens, but was becoming more prominent. She'd attended church as a child, but only read all the way through the Bible's initial five books for the first time in 1950, when the Laurences were delayed in Holland, waiting for their boat to take them to Africa. After she ran out of other reading material, she started reading the Gideon Bible in her hotel room. She was eventually struck by the parallels between the children of Israel and Somalis, both people of the desert, but she was especially drawn to Exodus 23:9—"Thou shalt not oppress a stranger, for ye know the heart of a stranger, seeing ye were strangers in the land of Egypt." It resonated for years after as she became a stranger in many lands. She also called her 1976 collection of articles *Heart of a Stranger*.

Laurence began contemplating other religions and comparing them to hers. She studied the Koran, Islam, and old religions in Africa, and Roman Catholicism when she rewrote *This Side Jordan* in Vancouver, and the Somalis' faith made her see her own religion with new eyes. She learned that Islam meant "submission to God" and that the Somalis always said, "In sha'Allah"—if Allah wills—regardless of whether it applied to whether they received rain or even lived. Laurence believed that kind of faith brought meaning to their suffering, and she compared their lives to hers: "Our lives had placed us in very few situations in which we had been virtually powerless.... Individualism and self-reliance had been woven into us all our lives. The total subservience of the individual judgement went against our deepest grain."[1] She even compared their two faiths: "I had never needed it the way they did. I viewed it from the outside. As far as I was concerned, God was deaf. If we did not hear the sound of each other's voices, no one else would."[2]

Laurence's cynicism was interesting because it contrasted to other spiritual moments in her life. She saw her son, David, the moment that he was born, and later wrote, "I felt as though I were looking over God's shoulder at the moment of the creation of life."[3] She enrolled him in a United Church play school and taught the Unitarian Sunday school in Vancouver, where she wrote a Christmas pageant that later became her second children's book, *The Christmas Birthday*

Story. Her African work was laced with religious references as she portrayed the clashes between Christianity and Africa's old religions and the Christian missions and modern education. *The Stone Angel* also showed Hagar's struggle with her father's religion and a minister as ineffectual as Laurence's was when her dad died. She used Biblical allusions—*This Side Jordan* is from Joshua 1:14–15 and the name Hagar is from Genesis 16. She even wrote to McClelland in 1963—when he wanted her to change the title of her first Canadian novel, *Hagar*—that she'd searched the Psalms for a new title because she felt "a great deal of the spirit of Presbyterianism in a way of Hagar herself is to be found there."[4] She eventually changed the book's name to *The Stone Angel* because of the image in its opening paragraph.

The second shift was that, as with many Canadians, Laurence's concern about nuclear survival was increasing in the early 1960s. It had only been a vague reference in her 1945 letters, but she wrote Wiseman in 1962: "I don't think there is much doubt that we are going to blow ourselves to pieces one of these days."[5] She also wrote in *The Prophet's Camel Bell*: "Looking at Amoud, and then at the nomads' huts crouched at the bottom of the hills, I could not help thinking of the western world with its power and its glory, its skyscrapers and its atom bombs, and wondering if these desert men would not after all survive longer than we did."[6]

What was undergoing the most change, however, was her

personal life. Laurence had been stressed for a while about trying to balance her roles as wife, mother, and writer, but Jack's frustration grew with her success because he wanted a more traditional wife. By 1962, she had tension headaches and prickling in her limbs, so she scaled back all of her work but writing. But their marital strain climaxed as Jack began to look for work overseas. She wrote Elliott that they were trying to sort out what each wanted to do in life, but it was complicated: "[H]e may be going abroad again, and I know that is right for him, but I wonder if I can become a memsahib once more?"

Laurence's drinking also escalated as she tried to cope. Biographer King said that it began in Neepawa when the girls used to consume the Crawford's liquor and refill the bottles with water. The Laurences drank socially in Somaliland and made wine in Vancouver, but King said that when she got drunk on the Gold Coast, she'd talk "incessantly about her family, particularly her grandfather's horrible behaviour."[7] During her first fall in B.C., Laurence's mum died, Jack had an operation, her family caught the flu, and the *Atlantic* rejected her novel. She wrote Wiseman: "I guess I hit the bottle pretty hard, & I swear that's the only way I got through those weeks."[8] In January 1963, she wrote again, noting that after she showed Jack *The Stone Angel*, she spent a year trying "to convince myself that I must be wrong about that novel, because if I weren't wrong, it indicated a lack of communication, on the personal level, which I had long known to be the case but which I simply could not face except in my solitary late-night sessions with the wine jug."[9]

The tension finally boiled over. Laurence later said that she didn't want to show Jack *The Stone Angel* because "I think I knew his response would be pivotal in our marriage." He insisted, but then didn't like it, even though, she wrote: "[F]or me it was the most important book I had written."[10] Her frustration from fifteen years of trying to avoid his disapproval finally spilled over, and in August 1962, they clashed over their personal differences and his criticism of her novel. She told Wiseman that she refused to go overseas with him, saying she'd take the children to England. She later said they each had to pursue their vocation, but it was hard for him to understand that writing was hers when all she had to show for her efforts were one published novel and having *The Prophet's Camel Bell* accepted for publication. She hoped they could work it out, but she felt that it was time to end her delayed adolescence. She also finally felt free of the despair that she'd felt for years.

King said the Laurences's separation was complicated by her affair with a Barbados writer, George Lamming. She'd just met him in Vancouver that August and wrote Wiseman that he was "Not only a very talented writer, but the kind of personality that hits you like the spirit of god between the eyes."[11] King reported that she followed him to England, hoping their relationship would continue, but her other biographer, Powers, said Lamming didn't even remember her.

In the fall of 1962, Jack left for East Pakistan to become an irrigation engineer. Margaret moved to England in mid-October with great hopes for the future. She was finally publishing, and now she wanted to find a writing community. She later said: "I imagined, wrongly as it turned out, there would be a literary community that would receive me with open arms and I would at last have the company of other writers, members of my tribe."[12]

CHAPTER 18

SETTLING IN ENGLAND

Laurence and her children arrived in England in late October 1964, after renting out their house in Vancouver and visiting Wiseman in Winnipeg. They immediately found a flat in Hampstead, the area that she knew and liked best. The flat was the top two floors of a Victorian brick house, close to the hospital where Jocelyn had been born. As in a prairie town, it was also near shops, services, and schools. The rooms were small, but every family member had a bedroom, though they soon found the flat was impossible to heat. But when Laurence wrote her friend, Gordon Elliott, on November 1, 1962, she said: "I am so glad to be here that all I can do in the evenings is walk around the flat and gloat about it. A room of one's own. Am I selfish? Yes. But I needed this place so badly, and I found it—a kind of divine dispensation. We are going to be okay."

Despite her elation, Laurence's fourteen months in London were tough. She arrived knowing that she had to be self-supporting in a year, though Jack covered their rent and food.

She soon discovered costs had increased and it was hard to make an income. She asked Macmillan for *The Prophet's Camel Bell* advance, then had to get back the tax the publisher deducted. The Canada Council rejected her application and she applied for several jobs, but found she was only qualified to be a typist and that didn't pay enough for child care. She later wrote: "I can never be that frightened again. I had literally never been on my own before."[1] Her children, aged ten and seven, helped her to keep going, but she wrote Elliot that half the time she felt pretty good and the "other half I feel depressed, miserable, lonely, bereft, empty, and just plain bloody awful."[2]

Laurence discovered that she was a survivor in February 1963 when she read in the paper about American writer Sylvia Plath's suicide. Plath was only six years younger, but they were both separated, writing, and living with two kids in the same area of Hampstead. Laurence later said she didn't believe those conditions caused Plath's death, as the suicide theme already ran through all of Plath's work. But she noted that she reacted differently than Plath when faced with the same conditions: "I found strengths I never knew I possessed, strengths that had probably been given to me by all my mothers."[3]

Seeing the doors slam shut, Laurence settled into the one thing she could do—write. Alan Maclean, a Macmillan director who became a friend, suggested that he might take her African short story collection. She revised it and Macmillan agreed at the end of 1962 to publish it as *The Tomorrow-*

Tamer. She then told Maclean she wanted to write several Canadian stories and a novel, but he suggested that she first rewrite *The Stone Angel.* Her luggage had been overweight when she visited Wiseman in Winnipeg, so she'd tossed her manuscript into a box with David's Meccano set, Jocelyn's books, and some tennis shoes, and mailed it to London, then agonized for five weeks: "This was the novel for which I had separated from my husband and embarked on who knew what, uprooting and dragging along my two children, and I almost seemed to be trying to lose it."4 By the time it arrived, she'd started rewriting the novel based on Jack's critique, but then decided not to proceed with his suggestions. As she wrote Wiseman: "It was better the first time. I'm not trying to write an historical novel, after all. What the hell do I care when they were using steam tractors on the prairies?" Realizing that she was trying to broaden its appeal by turn- ing it into something it wasn't, she decided to stick with her first draft because "[t]he old lady [Hagar] knew what she was doing when she told me her life story."5 She finished it on New Year's Eve, and again wrote Wiseman: "This novel means such a hell of a lot to me, simply because it is me."6 When Macmillan accepted it in 1963, she wrote: "I feel as though my faith in life, in myself, in everything, has been miraculously restored to me."7

The Prophet's Camel Bell and *The Tomorrow-Tamer* were published in Canada and England in 1963 and *The Stone*

Angel in 1964. Alfred Knopf published all three in New York in an unprecedented splash in 1964, and Laurence later thanked McClelland for persuading Knopf to publish her since that was a major turning point in her career. But she was still struggling to make a living and wrote in January 1963: "It is bloody awful that a writer can't earn a living from writing."[8] She read manuscripts for Macmillan, wrote radio scripts for the BBC African Service, and eventually did BBC book reviews. She even tried to do five-minute talks for the BBC *Women's Hour*, but gave up after discovering that she couldn't write unless her heart was in it. It was a blow because she was a slow writer and needed the money. She still wrote six stories that fall, most while vacationing with Jack in India. Her agent sold one to *Ladies' Home Journal* and she sold one to *Tamarack Review* and another to Macmillan for its 1963 *Winter's Tales*.

At the end of 1963, Laurence and her kids moved into the home they would occupy for the next decade. It was Elm Cottage near Penn in Buckinghamshire and close to London's airport. Maclean, her friend from Macmillan, showed it to them because it was empty after his mum died. They fell in love with it, glad to leave their London flat, though the rambling five-bedroom house with its tiny, low-ceilinged rooms was also cold. It was set on two-thirds of an acre with an overgrown garden. Laurence liked being able to have many guests, but still retain the privacy of her bedroom.

She'd decided she wanted to stay in England, preferably on her own since she was no longer a nervous wreck, so she signed a year's lease. She still wasn't sure how she'd support herself, but she rented a room to a boarder. Her family didn't like it any more than she had when her mum took in a boarder while she was a kid. But, by November 1968, she said: "I do love this place more than I can remember loving any other place except the house I was born in."9

Laurence liked living near Penn, even though she found she'd always be an outsider. As she later told *Chatelaine*: "I'm really a country person, or a small-town person.... I can live in a city for a while, but eventually it really bugs me." She didn't drive—she'd tried in Africa, but was too scared to continue—but she could walk to Penn's shops or phone for delivery. She also found its people friendly, but soon discovered they'd never consider her one of the villagers.

Laurence continued to struggle to balance family and writing even though Jack was gone. She later said: "My chief difficulty ... was in splitting my heart and my time between my children and my work."10 At first, she said she had trouble allowing herself to write because "I'd been brought up in a society in which jobs such as washing the dishes, making the beds, and scrubbing the floors were valuable work for women; writing was not. What helped me change my priorities was that my writing, as well as being my vocation, had become a source of income."11 She also struggled with being present for her children while she was writing. She found it hard to concentrate with them around, although they knew not to disturb her, even though they hated how mentally and emotionally absent she was then. She found it equally hard to exit her fictional world and return to the real one, even though she stopped a few hours before they came home. She later said that once "inside that fictional world, it's extraordinarily difficult to get out, and what happens, I think, is that you simultaneously lead two lives. There comes a time when you are no longer sure of which one is the more real."[12] She'd sometimes take the children on outings and trips, but King reported that she was often explosive and in need of assurance, so life remained difficult for all of them.

Her marriage didn't fare much better. The Laurences seesawed for seven years before finally settling their relationship in 1969. She initially feared she'd have to join Jack overseas, but then he sold the Vancouver house in 1964 and made Elm Cottage his base. They separated in 1965, then tried reconciling, but Jack still wanted a traditional wife with him and Laurence felt the strain of juggling three roles. Jack even took an irrigation consultant's job and lived in a London suburb for awhile in 1967 while working overseas for months at a time. They reconciled in 1968, but Laurence said: "[T]he outer and inner were in constant conflict, and [the] result of that was the bottle, never before such a bad problem. Things improved when I quit drinking, but only because I could then suppress all and be what I wasn't."[13] Jack finally left for Swaziland in January 1969, and in May, wrote for a divorce as he'd found someone else. Laurence said they'd tried for two years, and if they couldn't be happy, she wanted to be free of the guilt for not being his kind of wife. But she was still devastated when the divorce was proclaimed just before Christmas 1969. King said that she locked herself in the bathroom after and threatened to kill herself, and by the time her children and friends coaxed her out, she'd taken enough pills that she slept for two days.

There could be many reasons for Laurence's vulnerability—being orphaned so young, the conflict of being a working woman in a conventional marriage before the rise of feminism, or even the fact that she was a sensitive writer struggling with life. No one could ever explain the roots of it, but she often felt lonely, guilty, or depressed—what she called her "black Celt" or "Celtic gloom." She was also frustrated that women writers had to work, raise kids, and do housework plus their own secretarial work, while male writers often had wives, and if they were academics, also secretaries. In 1967, she also said: "I wish I weren't so easily terrified by life."[14] She had tension-related accidents and health problems, and often drank to deal with her life. As she wrote Wiseman in 1965: "I cope with confusion so badly—when things get too hectic, I have about six stiff drinks and then I can take anything in my stride but afterwards I feel guilty as hell and worry lest I go the way of so many of our tribe."[15] There were times she wondered if she was an alcoholic, then decided she wasn't, but went on the wagon anyway. She even cleared the booze from her house in December 1968 and took pills to induce vomiting if she had a drink. The vulnerability that resulted in her drinking would always make her life difficult, but it was something that she would never overcome even after her writing success.

CHAPTER 19

THE GIFT OF GRACE

Laurence's years in England were professionally her most productive as she wrote six books, including her remaining Manawaka fiction. It was also an interesting spiritual time for she usually sensed something beyond her was helping her write. She'd struggled for years to answer her call and finally started seeing the results, which earned her some well-deserved accolades.

While she was still in Vancouver, Laurence started the book that would become two novels—*A Jest of God* and *The Fire-Dwellers*—before she began *The Stone Angel*. She restarted this book in December 1964 after writing some stories and articles, but it still wouldn't come the way *The Stone Angel* had. It was frustrating, and she said: "[T]his time the person is very evasive, and this is part of her, and very understandable, but she is damn well making life impossible for me. I think that the grace for which one hopes will not come, perhaps, this time. Lacking it, I don't see any way except to put down as simply and directly as possible the things that happen, and to try not to tell lies. I don't believe this is enough, but it appears to be all I have to hand at the moment."[1]

She eventually discovered that this new book was two novels, *A Jest of God* and *The Fire-Dwellers*, the stories of two Manawaka sisters who envied each others' lives one summer. She focused on *A Jest of God* and tried writing it various ways, then opened her notebook one morning and began "as I always have, as though taking down dictation."[2] She wrote Wiseman in 1965: "[T]he novel demands some kind of ability to tune into something which isn't conscious so much as intuitive, and for that you have to be a very attentive listener, which I couldn't be for awhile." She also made another discovery: "I can do a basically one-character novel with some truth."[3] This tale was of Rachel Cameron, thirty-four, an unmarried teacher in a small prairie town who lived with her invalid mother and didn't have the chance to have children. She took a Ukrainian lover, then thought she was pregnant and decided to cope with the town's censure even if an illegitimate birth caused a scandal. She found she wasn't pregnant, but her lover left and she started taking charge of her life.

A Jest of God's 1966 publication was a turning point for Laurence. She already had a reputation as a Commonwealth writer and the new Somaliland Republic even invited her to its independence celebration that year. She also began to gain North American recognition, which Jack McClelland capitalized on by arranging a five-city promotional tour. The Canada

Council gave her a travel grant and an arts fellowship to start her next novel. The ten-week tour was exhausting, but she returned to Canada in 1967 when *Jest* won the Governor-General's award. Paul Newman also made *Jest* into his first film, *Rachel, Rachel*, starring his wife, Joanne Woodward. Laurence earned enough from the award and film—$32,000—to write for eighteen months and buy Elm Cottage, which Maclean wanted to sell so he could marry and buy a house.

Laurence hated doing publicity, but the 1966 trip provided some important Manitoba moments. She enjoyed returning to Winnipeg that October, where Professor Walter Swayze had nominated her to become one of United College's honorary fellows. Bob Hallstead, her friend and former professor, supported the nomination and read her citation at the fall convocation while Swayze lectured on *A Jest of God*, which Jack McClelland had sent him as page proofs. Laurence was the first woman and youngest person to receive United College's honour, and it was the first of fourteen university recognitions and doctorates she eventually received. The University of Manitoba would award the last honorary degree to her in 1986, just months before she died.

While she was in Winnipeg, Hallstead pressed Laurence to return to Neepawa. It was an agonizing day, but a seminal one for her. Swayze said she didn't want to go, even though she hadn't been there since 1949, and she returned to Winnipeg visibly shaken. She later described her pilgrimage to several people. She wrote Canadian writer, Al Purdy, with whom she carried on a long correspondence, that she stood by her parents' graves and realized that if they still existed—"and they do, all the ancestors do"—then it was in her head.[4] She also told an interviewer that she wanted to see her grandfather's house "because this had symbolized him and symbolized my life as a child."[5] She found it was solid, but not as vast as she remembered. She wrote about that experience in "Jericho's Brick Battlements," her last *A Bird in the House* story, which was a fictionalized autobiography that portrayed her sitting in the car outside the house: "I had not thought it would hurt me to see it in other hands, but it did. I wanted to tell them to trim their hedges, to repaint the windowframes, to pay heed to repairs. I had feared and fought the old man, yet he proclaimed himself in my veins."[6] She also told Lyall Powers, well before he wrote her biography, that she "could never have finished that collection if I hadn't gone back to Neepawa that summer."[7]

Laurence had also finished another book before going to Canada in 1966. It was *Long Drums and Cannons*, her survey of Nigeria's contemporary English literature. She'd met several young Nigerian writers through friends in London in 1965 and produced four BBC scripts on West Africa. She spent months on those and then the producer changed his request, so she wrote the book to salvage what she learned because, she noted, "I found it exciting that African writers were producing what I and many Canadian writers were producing: a truly non-colonial literature."[8] She'd also discovered the same thing Nigerian novelist Chinua Achebe had, which was that "when you write about your own people and place you write about things you did not know you knew whereas if you are writing about another country you have not got all that background."[9] The book was hard to write, but she liked the fact that the Africans were exploring their societies, backgrounds, and people to seek "links with the ancestors and the old gods in order to discover who they themselves were."[10] Macmillan published the book to little fanfare in 1968, but it gained her further African recognition. She was particularly praised by Achebe and other Nigerian writers, who found her book much wiser than did her Canadian critics. In an interesting parallel to what she learned from reading Sinclair Ross's *As For Me and My House* in Neepawa, several African writers later said that her writing showed them they could also write about their own experience.

When Laurence returned to England after her 1966 and 1967 travels, she received another book by grace. She noted that *Jason's Quest* "came—all in a piece, complete, package deal. Come to think of it, nearly everything I've ever written has come that way."[11] It was a children's book based on the moles that she'd exterminated for digging two-foot hills in her lawn. The story was about Jason, a mole, an owl, and two cats named after her cats, Topaz and Calico, who travelled to London to search for a cure for the malaise destroying their community. They found the cure, but also learned about their prejudices. It was the only book she wrote from her English context. Macmillan accepted it after a rewrite and published it in 1970 to less than glowing reviews.

Laurence then returned to struggling with *The Fire-Dwellers*. She'd been working on it since 1960, and it initially scared her because it reminded her so much of herself. As she said in 1965: "I kept telling myself the character wasn't me, yet when the circumstances of my life changed, the plot changed, and she *would* persist in speaking in my voice."[12] She abandoned the book again because it was too complex, but said that she'd learned a lot about herself. For one thing, she had the same deep puritanical inhibitions about self-revelation that she'd had with *The Prophet's Camel Bell*. She said: "I cannot ever speak the truth when I am speaking in my own voice ... Only when the character is quite different from myself." She also found that she had such a shaky sense of her own reality that hardly anything she said in her voice seemed true to her, and she was only reasonably certain when she'd "temporarily become someone else."[13] Finally, she wrote that she realized she always told placating lies, except to "the few members of my tribe whom I trust absolutely.[14] It was the same sense of niceness that troubled her with *The Prophet's Camel Bell*.

When Laurence began writing *The Fire-Dwellers* again in 1967, she was appalled by its multiple threads. It was the tale of Stacey MacAindra, thirty-nine, a middle-aged WASP housewife and mother of four who lived in Vancouver. Stacey struggled to communicate with her non-verbal husband, Mac, and both their kids and their parents. She tried to accept her life's irreversibility, and she took a lover in the midst of her chaos as she tried to make some peace with her life. She also lived in fear of raising her kids in an increasingly violent world.

Laurence struggled to convey the incoherence of Stacey's jangled life. She finally burnt the hundreds of pages and plans that she'd collected for the book over the years and started again. She could feel the novel lurking just beyond her grasp and wrote Wiseman: "What I really need is a kind of gift from my personal protector-god (my concepts of this become progressively more African as the years go by)—what I need is grace."[15] That grace never came, but she kept trying to achieve TV's audiovisual effect and contrast what Stacey said with what she thought. The old narrative methods didn't work, and she considered writing two columns with the "inner and outer going on simultaneously, side by side on the page—fine if you had a two-foot wide page and a reader with four eyes."[16] In the struggle to portray what she wanted, she pared text, dropped quotation marks, and used italics and unusual alignment, but still found it a dim appropriation. By December 1976, *The Fire-Dwellers* was finally well underway, but she said: "I don't dare look back at what I've written, or like Lot's wife, I will be turned into a pillar of salt."[17]

Laurence finally finished *The Fire-Dwellers* in the spring of 1968, then agonized over whether anyone would want to read about a middle-aged housewife. She was relieved when the publishers—Macmillan in England and McClelland and Stewart in Canada—accepted it since Stacey presented a dilemma that she'd felt, which was living in the past while trying to face herself as mother to a new generation. The book was written in her generation's voice and showed her concerns, from a failing marriage to nuclear destruction. Laurence said: "I was fed up with the current fictional portraits of women of my generation—middle-aged mums either being presented as glossy magazine types, perfect, everloving and incontestably contented, or else as sinister and spiritually cannibalistic monsters determined only to destroy their men and kids by hypnotic means."[18] *The Fire-Dwellers* was heralded by a *Time* article and *Ladies' Home Journal* serialization, but it was published in 1969 to mixed reviews. People either sympathized with Stacey or hated her, and Laurence said some of the most vitriolic reviews came from middle-aged men who might have a wife like Stacey at home. Stunned, she said, "Jesus—I never meant to threaten anybody!!!"[19]

Laurence returned to the stories she'd been writing for *A Bird in the House* since 1962. She'd published the first, "The Sound of the Singing," in *Winter's Tales* in 1963, a year before *The Stone Angel* was released. Since then, she'd published others in a later edition of *Winter's Tales*, the *Ladies' Home*

Journal, Atlantic Monthly, Atlantic Advocate, Argosy, and *Chatelaine.* She always said these were her most autobiographical tales because their heroine, Vanessa MacLeod, retold many of her experiences. Each story followed a thread, including her father's death and her experience with a cousin who stayed with them, then went to war, but the stories were saturated with Neepawa's people and places. The most prominent was Grandfather Connor, who displayed many of her grandfather's characteristics, though he never rocked in the basement. Laurence later said that she disliked her grandfather throughout the stories, but "when I'd finished the last story I realized not only that I didn't dislike him anymore, but that there were things about him that I greatly admired."[20] She originally planned ten stories, but only wrote eight and always envisioned them as separate, with the interrelated effect of a novel. When Laurence finished, Knopf's editor Judith Jones tried to convince her to turn the collection into a novel to improve sales. She refused, believing that would ruin the stories. Knopf finally agreed to let the stories stand, but paid her a lower advance, and *A Bird in the House* was published in 1970.

The end of the 1960s marked the close of an era. Laurence had finished all but one of her novels and seen many changes in the preceding decade. In 1969, she summed up the decade by saying:

I have become more involved with novels of character and with trying to feel how it would be to *be* that particular person. My viewpoint has altered from modified optimism to modified pessimism. I have become more concerned with form in writing than I used to be. I have moved closer (admittedly, in typically cautious stages) to an expression of my idiom and way of thought.... I've listened to the speech of three generations—my grandparents, my parents and my own, and maybe I've even heard what some of it means....

At the moment, I have the same feeling as I did when I knew I had finished writing about Africa. I've gone as far as I personally can go, in the area in which I've lived for the past three novels. A change of direction would appear to be indicated. I have a halfway hunch where I want to go, but I don't know how to get there or what will be there if I do. Maybe I'll strike it lucky and find the right compass, or maybe I won't.[21]

CHAPTER 20

CHECKING OUT CANADA

By the spring of 1969, Laurence was beginning to move on with her life. Jack had asked for a divorce, finally freeing her from their perpetual dance. She loved Elm Cottage in England, but had been toying with the idea of returning to Canada, knowing that she could take the proceeds from her house sale and resettle there. She'd also been waiting for her children to finish school, and they were almost done and ready to move on, too. An opportunity arose to point her back to her homeland, and she was eager to explore it to see if she really wanted to live there again.

This watershed occurred when Laurence had the chance to become the University of Toronto's (U. of T.) writer-in-residence for 1969–70. Wiseman asked her about it in 1967. Public speaking terrified Laurence—she shook so much that she finally learned at U. of T. to sit at a table. But she'd given a couple of lectures in England, so she said she'd consider it because she felt isolated, needed to hear Canadians' inflection and idiom again, wanted to talk to young writers, and also wanted to see how she liked Toronto. She figured she'd have to move there to earn a living. She also wanted to earn enough to buy some property. As she later wrote: "I needed the money, I needed the clout, or thought I did, and I felt I needed the experience."[1]

Once she agreed, an interesting number of Manitoba connections helped to seal the appointment. Wiseman talked to their former professor, Malcolm Ross. Then Jack Sword— a Saskatchewan boy who'd been raised in Winnipeg, married Laurence's high-school teacher, Connie Offen, and become U. of T.'s acting president—offered her the job. Another one of Laurence's friends, Don Cameron, who'd just joined the faculty at Halifax's Dalhousie University, was trying to arrange a similar appointment there. Laurence initially preferred that smaller city and institution, but was still trying to stabilize her marriage when the Dalhousie opportunity arose in 1968. She declined it and accepted the U. of T. post a year later.

Laurence started her U. of T. post in September 1969. She feared that she wouldn't have any students for eight months, so, ever the Scots Presbyterian, she plastered the campus with posters, then had to turn away the public to have enough time for students. She only had to give a couple of public lectures each term, but felt that she needed to earn her keep, so she regularly met with students, attended Canadian literature classes, and spoke to a diverse range of groups, including the University Women's Clubs and engineering students who wanted to talk about women. She even travelled to McGill and several Maritime universities since she'd rejected Dalhousie's offer. By March 1970, she hadn't written in a year and was tired of answering the public's requests to read their manuscripts and tell them how to get published. She also questioned what good she was doing the students since she'd met only a few promising writers. As she wrote Al Purdy: "Like, the kids who are any good do not NEED any help or encouragement, of COURSE. And those who ain't—what can you do but be tactful?"[2] She finished the position psychically drained.

While Laurence was at U. of T., she received another Manitoban's invitation that led her to Trent University and the Peterborough area that would eventually become her home. In September 1969, Peg Morton, the wife of Manitoba historian W.L. (Bill) Morton, who'd been at Trent for five years, invited her to speak to the Trent University Women's Club. Laurence agreed because she remembered meeting Bill—who was from Gladstone, near Neepawa—when she was sixteen. She said he was nineteen when some boys came home for Christmas holidays, and he drove while his friend necked with Laurence's best friend in the back seat. "I was dragged along as company for him," she wrote Purdy. "I was petrified of Morton—he seemed a million miles away, and so bored with a 16 year old Neepawa girl he could hardly stay awake to drive the car. What a laugh. I will remind him."[3]

It's hard to know how accurate Laurence's memory of

Morton was since, by the time she was sixteen in 1942, Morton was a Rhodes Scholar eighteen years her senior who had just started teaching at the University of Manitoba (U. of M.). But her biographer, Powers, said she spoke to the Trent University Women's Club about how her prairie background influenced her writing. That essay appeared in the 1970 Manitoba centennial edition of the University of Manitoba's *Mosaic* and later became the lead essay in *A Place to Stand On*. Laurence said in a tribute to Morton when he died and she followed him as Trent's chancellor that she stayed with the Mortons in 1969 and "discovered Trent was a small and excellent liberal arts university of the type I most admired. This was indeed a factor in my ultimately settling in this area."[4]

Laurence arrived in Canada wanting to buy property. When I met her in 1978, she said: "My aim was to save enough money so I could buy a little cottage somewhere in this country to get a foothold because I always knew I wanted to move back." Cottages were part of her history as her family had had one at Clear Lake and the Laurences had bought one in Washington in 1961. She'd originally considered buying a Toronto house with rooms for tenants and a shack on a nearby lake so she could connect with her "tribe," but still preserve some of her privacy for writing. But, after visiting the Mortons in the fall of 1969, she found a three-bedroom cedar fishing shack, which she called the "Manawaka" cottage. It was on the Otonabee River, five miles south of Peterborough, and its large picture window overlooked the river that appeared to flow both ways. She put up posters of her heroes, Louis Riel and Norman Bethune, and delighted in furnishing it from the Eaton's catalogue: "For a prairie person growing up in the thirties and forties, one universal fantasy had always been to be able to order anything you wanted from the Eaton's or Hudson's Bay Company catalogue."[5] She spent several summers writing *The Diviners* and entertaining friends at her cottage, though she sometimes left for friends' places in Toronto when she had too much company to write. She sold the cottage in 1980, noting it was too much to keep up two places. She'd also found that she could no longer write there: "I think in my mind the river at that place was too much connected with the writing of *The Diviners*."[6]

CHAPTER 21

THE DIVINERS

By the time she returned to England in 1970, Laurence knew she had one novel left to write. She didn't know it then, but *The Diviners* would mark the pinnacle of her life's work. It built on the themes she had developed in her African and Canadian writing, but also allowed her to express her unique voice and approach her prairie roots from a new perspective.

Laurence first tried to write an African novel in the fall of 1970. It was an allegorical tale set in a mythical West African country, an idea that she'd had since 1962. She was bored with traditional realism and had tried to get away from it in her previous two novels. She restarted the new book a dozen times, trying different forms and voices, but as with her earlier failed novels, it grew too complicated and scared her when it started to resemble her life too closely. She finally realized in March 1971 that she'd been writing the wrong book since she'd outgrown the need to do another African novel and felt there was a new Canadian one growing under its surface. She wrote: "What I was avoiding was the necessity of coming closer to home, closer to myself."[1] She tossed out six months of work, finding she'd tried "to write a theory as a novel, which will *never* work for me. As a theory it was great; as a novel it was dead before it even began."[2]

In the spring of 1971, Laurence said: "I woke up with a thought in my mind. I took a notebook out to the lawn and began to write a novel that I knew even then would be called *The Diviners*. It felt as though I had been waiting for it, and it had been waiting for me. I couldn't write it fast enough."[3] She wasn't sure what it was about, but it was long and complicated: "I felt a great need to use a variety of techniques, simply to try to get across a whole lot of different things."[4] She worked on the novel for two years, sometimes fearing that it would quit before she finished. It was one of the most difficult and exhausting things she ever did, and Swayze said it almost killed her. When she finally finished in February 1973, she knew that it needed revising, but was too tired to do it. Knopf editor Judith Jones visited Laurence before she moved to Canada in July 1973 and they spent six hours discussing what needed to be done to the book. Biographer King said that when Jones saw the manuscript, "she was convinced of two things: it bore the mark of genius and it was an utter mess."[5] The text had to be severely cut and Laurence finished the revisions before she started her next university residency in Canada that fall.

Laurence always called *The Diviners* a spiritual autobiography, as it expressed her voice, thought, and passions. It was the story of mid-career writer, Morag Gunn, an orphan raised in a small prairie town by the garbage collector and his wife. It was a complex tale that examined her life and relationships growing up in Manawaka, the prejudice that she felt and also experienced, and her journey as she claimed her life as a writer. Gunn left her husband to pursue her writing, but did it by taking a Métis lover, Jules Tonnerre, whom she knew growing up. The book included both of their cultural pasts— the stories of Manitoba's Scots pioneers and Métis—the sense of them being dispossessed people in the present, and the future promise for their daughter, Pique.

The Diviners was published in 1974 to mixed reviews. Some praised its brilliance while others hated its innovative format. Laurence included the past, present, and future by using different techniques. She especially explored the concept of time since she'd come to believe "the past and the future are both always present."[6] By then, she felt that a story's present time must "include not only the totality of the characters' lives but also the inherited time of perhaps two or even three past generations, in terms of parents' and grandparents' recollections, and the much much longer past which has become legend, the past of a collective cultural memory."[7]

Laurence tried to enhance the sense of past, present, and future in *The Diviners* by using descriptions of snapshots, tales, memory bank movies, and songs. She was particularly proud of the social protest songs that she wrote, which provided Jules Tonnerre with a way to communicate what he couldn't say in the novel. Music had always been part of her life—she even loved singing labour songs in Winnipeg in the 1940s and listening to the youth's folk songs at her home in England. She noted that writing the songs "was testing the limits of my own abilities to convey stuff as a writer."[8] But she was particularly excited when a Canadian graduate student, Ian Cameron, visited her and set her words to the tunes she hummed, and she finally convinced Jack McClelland to make a promotional record of the songs for *The Diviners*. She even joined the Composers, Authors, and Publishers Association of Canada, thinking she might have a new career after she finished writing.

The Diviners advanced the theme that she'd been developing through her writing. While her African work was about freedom—a natural outgrowth of Ghana's independence movement—her Manawaka books were about survival. She later said: "I didn't know I was changing so much when I wrote *The Stone Angel*.... Perhaps I no longer believed so much in the promised land, even the promised land of one's own inner freedom."[9] In her books, Hagar introduced the survival theme as she wanted to survive with dignity until death. Rachel in *A Jest of God* and Stacey in *The Fire-Dwellers* were threatened by their past and inadequacies, and Laurence said each found "within herself an ability to survive—not just to go on living, but to change and to move into new areas of life."[10] The survival theme also reflected Laurence's life as it resonated in her work:

> My writing, then, has been my own attempt to come to terms with the past. I see this process as the gradual one of freeing oneself from the stultifying aspect of the past, while at the same time beginning to see its true value— which, in the case of my own people (by which I mean the total community, not just my particular family), was a determination to survive against whatever odds.
>
> The theme of survival—not just physical survival, but the preservation of some human dignity and in the end some human warmth and ability to reach out and touch others—this is, I have come to think, an almost inevitable theme for a writer such as I, who came from a Scots-Irish background of stern values and hard work and puritanism, and who grew up during the drought and depression of the thirties and then the war.[11]

While Laurence's previous Manawaka novels were each about an individual, *The Diviners* reached beyond that to the tribe. She'd grown fascinated with Africa's tribal concept, then began exploring her ancestry after she wrote *The Stone Angel* and found she harboured mixed feelings about the Manitoba pioneers, especially her grandparents. She noted that she hadn't realized "how difficult they were to live with, how authoritarian, how unbending, how afraid to show love, many of them, and how willing to show anger. And yet, they had inhabited a wilderness and made it fruitful. They were, in the end, great survivors, and for that I love and value them."[12] Then, when she was writing about the African writers in *Long Drums and Cannons*, she added: "I began to see how much my own writing had followed the same pattern—the attempt to assimilate the past, partly in order to be freed from it, partly in order to try to understand myself and perhaps others of my generation, through seeing where we had come from."[13]

Laurence's interest in ancestors created two major streams in *The Diviners*—the stories that Morag's adoptive father, Christie, told her about her Scottish past, and the stories that Jules relayed about his Métis heritage. Laurence grew up with a strong sense of her Scottish ancestry and made several trips to Scotland while living in England. She visited the Lowland Scots area of her father's Wemyss family, but was more fascinated with the Highland Scots who were stripped of their land and exiled, as were Africa's slaves. She loved Scotland, but left feeling that part of her heritage was "Mock Scots" as her real roots were with the Scottish immigrants in Manitoba and not the people of Scotland. She later said: "I knew then where I belonged, which was in that small prairie town in Manitoba."[14] The result was she ended that pilgrimage with "a sense of the wheel coming full circle, that kind of journey, where we end up in the place where we began, but with a different perspective."[15] Laurence then started tracing the story of the Scottish settlers who travelled to Manitoba after the 1800s Highland clearances. They journeyed by ship through Hudson Bay to northern Manitoba, then to the Red River settlement, which is now Winnipeg. She always wanted to see the area of northern Manitoba through which they travelled, but there is no record that she did. Still, her discoveries about her Scottish ancestry and the realization of where she really belonged formed part of the framework that anchored *The Diviners*.

The Métis presence in *The Diviners* also grew from Laurence's interest in them as a dispossessed people. There weren't many Métis in Neepawa when she was growing up, but she became intrigued by them while living in Africa. She felt drawn to Louis Riel, and Clara Thomas wrote that Laurence found a sympathetic account of both the Scottish settlers and Métis when she read W.L. Morton's *Manitoba: A History* the summer that she started writing *The Diviners*.[16] Laurence incorporated some of Manitoba's history as part of Jules's Métis heritage. She particularly emphasized the story of Louis Riel's rebellion against the Dominion government as the Province of Manitoba was formed in 1870 and the Métis's uprising in Batoche was in 1885.

By the mid-1960s, Laurence was already drawing parallels among these three dispossessed people—the African tribes,

Scots clans, and Canadian Métis. She wrote essays, including "The Poem and the Spear" in 1964 and "Road from the Isles" for *Maclean's* in 1968. These noted that all three societies had been dispossessed by British imperialism. As she wrote:

> What one has come to see, in the last decade, is that tribalism is an inheritance of us all. Tribalism is not such a bad thing, if seen as the bond which an individual feels with his roots, his ancestors, his background. It may or may not be stultifying in a personal sense, but that is a problem each of us has to solve or not solve. Where tribalism becomes, to my mind, frighteningly dangerous is where the tribe—whatever it is, the Hausa, the Ibo, the Scots Presbyterians, the Daughters of the American Revolution, the in-group—is seen, as "the people," the human beings, and the others, the un-tribe, are seen as sub-human. This is not Africa's problem alone; it is everyone's.[17]

It is interesting that her description of tribalism also denoted life in a small prairie town. From my experience, I knew that community bonding could be good when it connected people to each other, and many were comforted by that, but it could also be very destructive when it excluded those who were different, making them feel like lesser people.

After writing *The Diviners*, Laurence left her fiction career with a new understanding of her past and her ancestors. She said that the survival theme was not just personal, but Canadian, as everyone had to find a way to live with his or her own past. But, she also noted: "[A]fter a certain time, *the ancestors* are everyone's ancestors—mine, in some ways, are not only the Scots but also the Métis; I was born in a land which they had inhabited, shaped and invested with their ghosts."[18] The wheel had come full circle and she had returned to her prairie roots with a new understanding, and was now ready to embrace her future.

CHAPTER 22

ROOTS AND WINGS

Laurence's life in England made little impact on her writing, but it reinforced the Canadian roots from which she built her life and legacy. She learned some useful publishing information and gained a sense of other nations' writing, but she wrote: "I don't really believe my being here has influenced my writing one way or another, certainly not to anything like the same extent as Africa once did."[1] What she said she found instead was that "my way of seeing, however much it may have changed over the years, remains in some enduring way that of a small-town prairie person."[2]

The most obvious tie between Laurence's prairie past and Canadian writing was Manawaka, the Manitoba setting of her Canadian fiction. She was a teen living in Neepawa when she created its name for her first unpublished novel, *The Land of Our Fathers*. When the name re-emerged with *The Stone Angel*, she never dreamed that it would anchor her remaining fiction. While she was writing, she always insisted that "Manawaka is not my hometown of Neepawa—it has elements of Neepawa, especially in some of the descriptions of places," but she sometimes added that it was "not so much any one prairie town as an amalgam of many prairie towns."[3] Unlike my family, which moved around, Laurence never lived in any other prairie communities, so she never realized that each one had a distinct heritage and personality. Neepawa's historian, Cecil Pittman, also showed me the various local settings that were in her books—the elite's brick houses, the "flats" area by the river that the poor people inhabited, the family funeral home, and the location of the trestle bridge. Laurence finally admitted to University of Manitoba professors David Arnason and Dennis Cooley months before she died that "the fictional town of Manawaka was based to a very large extent on my childhood memories of my own town of Neepawa." Still, it remained a town of her mind and she wrote Purdy that it was odd to see it come alive in Paul Newman's film, *Rachel, Rachel*. Walter Swayze told me that Newman couldn't raise the money to film *Rachel, Rachel* in Manitoba, so he filmed it in Connecticut so he could board the cast and crew in his home and make day trips to shoot. "Having spent four years in Connecticut," said Swayze, "I was probably more disturbed than most by the differences between the movie and the novel."

Manawaka was probably Canadian literature's most famous fictional town. It was built up over five books of layered characters and geography, but Laurence said that it was "a microcosm of the larger world ... everything that happens everywhere else in some way or other, in some shape or form, happens there because this is society."[4] She mined its local veins to portray the universal, and many readers felt that they were Stacey or that Hagar resembled their grandmother. Laurence also included other settings, though none as comprehensive as Manawaka. *The Stone Angel* had Vancouver's abandoned cannery and the senile old woman who brought Laurence a bedpan while she was in hospital there, and *The Fire-Dwellers* was rife with Vancouver settings. The stone angel may even have been modelled after the marble angel monuments Laurence saw in Genoa, Italy's, Staglieno cemetery on her way to Africa, since she told an interviewer in 1981 that she wasn't thinking of Neepawa's stone angel when she wrote that book.[5] *Jason's Quest* included references to Laurence's English cats, address, and local train stations. *The Diviners* was also laced with Peterborough elements: the Otonabee River that flowed both ways and the swallows that swept it outside of Laurence's cottage window; Catharine Parr Traill, the pioneer writer she admired who had lived in the area; and the diviner who marked Laurence's cottage well. But their impact was not as far-reaching as Manawaka's, and once Laurence was finished writing about it, she said that she felt an emptiness, for part of her inner dwelling place was gone.

Laurence's life in England also showed some interesting spiritual shifts from the time she left the prairies. She moved as far from organized religion as she ever got and stopped going to church. She'd attended a Unitarian church in Vancouver and there was one near her London flat, but she noted right after she arrived in England that she hadn't gone yet: "[T]hey seem a little too cheery and positive thinking for my frame of mind."[6] She wanted to find a Coptic church while visiting Egypt for Christmas 1966, but by the end of the 1960s, she described herself as a religious agnostic. She even told a CBC interviewer in 1969: "I was a religious atheist and writing was my way of praying."[7] She also explained to *Chatelaine* soon after that: "I have some kind of faith, but not with a traditional church. But I value the myths and rituals of religion. I think they're necessary and reassuring to the human spirit." Laurence also believed life was a great mystery that didn't need solving and people couldn't define God, who left them free will.

Her personal spirituality also deepened during this period. She wrote friends asking them to pray for her to receive the grace with which she wrote. She told her former professor, Bob Hallstead, in 1966: "More and more I feel that a lot is in God's hands, not mine, and there is a kind of relief in this feeling." She also called writing an act of will and faith, and felt possessed when it was going well. She said her characters existed in another dimension and she had to pray hard to make contact with them, then try not to manipulate them. Over the years, she also developed a gift of knowing how many novels she had left to write. She called it her Celtic second sight as she counted down the ones that she felt still needed to be done.

Spiritual themes constantly appeared in her books, many of them resembling her views. *Long Drums and Cannons* examined the Christian undertone in Nigerian writing. *Jason's Quest* decried prejudice and lethargy, and her Manawaka books cited Biblical references and hymns. She said Hagar's pride "was spiritual pride, using it in the Christian sense of the seven deadly sins."[8] Laurence's characters argued with God, just as she did in her journals when she was dying, and Stacey was as contemptuous of Christian doctrine as Laurence was. Swayze said Christie of *The Diviners* was also a Christ-like figure, embodying the prophet Isaiah's suffering servant and taking away the sins of Manawaka. Clara Thomas finally wrote that all of Laurence's work was infused and unified by a "passion for a sustaining faith and wholeness.... On the deepest, dynamic level she is a religious novelist and all of her works are facets of one whole, a pilgrim's progress towards the complementary and intertwining knowledge of self and knowledge of God."[9]

Laurence's sense of justice continued to tie her work to her social gospel roots. She cast the socially marginal—an old woman, a spinster, a housewife, a garbage collector, the Métis, and even a writer—in her work and focused on each person's uniqueness. She later said that in the decade after she wrote her first novel, "I had had to abandon every *ism* except individualism and even that seemed a little creaky until the last syllable fully vanished of itself, leaving me ismless."[10] After she discovered her strength was portraying individuals, she said that she felt her work of proclaiming every individual unique and irreplaceable was "part of my Christian faith."[11] She showed those people's place in the social order and the prejudice—racial, class, or ethnic—that they encountered, often documenting life on the wrong side of the tracks. Even Morag realized she was wrong to be ashamed of the garbage collector who raised her. Laurence often didn't know a book's theme until it was half written, but Swayze said she was surprised how Christian it usually was. In 1968, she said that everything she'd written, from Africa to Canada, was concerned with the current social patterns, and she later noted it was all socially political.

The one discord that was cited about Laurence's work involved the Métis. She'd worried whether she got their voice right and said in her memoir that her Lakefield friend, Alice Olsen Williams, assured her she had. But Williams, an Anishinaabe, told me there'd been something disquieting about Laurence's Métis portraits. She then pulled out Janice Acoose's 1995 book, *Iskwewak*, in which Acoose said Piquette Tonnerre, the drunk and disorderly Métis woman that Laurence drew in "The Loons" in *A Bird in the House*, was "vaguely embarrassing."[12] The reference was disquieting because, looking back, Laurence's portrait read more like a stereotype, even though she was trying to point out the plight of Canada's Aboriginal and Métis people by addressing it in that story and including a reference to Piquette's demise again in *The Diviners*.

Laurence's other social concerns were reflected in her writing. War continued to run as a leitmotif through her fiction—the first war, in which her dad fought, and the second, that killed the Neepawa boys that she knew. She grew more concerned about the nuclear threat. Despite not seeing herself as a joiner, she joined the local Campaign for Nuclear Disarmament group when she moved to London in 1962 and was part of its 1963 protest march to Aldermaston, Berkshire, the site of the Atomic Energy Research Establishment's factory. Her fear of nuclear destruction informed Stacey's fear in *The Fire-Dwellers* and formed the basis of her 1964 science fiction story, "A Queen in Thebes," in which a mother and son survived a nuclear holocaust. This era heightened Laurence's sensitivity about the nuclear threat, which later manifested itself in her social activism.

Feminist sensitivities were also part of Laurence's work and life. She said it took a long time to find her voice as a woman writer. Even Miranda's birth scene in *This Side Jordan* was written from her husband's perspective. Laurence told Margaret Atwood in 1974 that, while her work dealt with many issues that women's liberation addressed, she hadn't realized until after her books were published how widespread her sentiments were: "My generation of women came to a lot of the same conclusions, but they did it in isolation."[13] Then she added that, while she was 90 percent in agreement with women's lib, people had to pay attention to the problems men would have dealing with the changes women were experiencing: "Men have to be reeducated with the minimum of damage to them. These are our husbands, our sons, our lovers ... we can't live without them, and we can't go to war against them. The change must liberate them as well."[14]

The other aspect that became obvious was the deeply autobiographical well from which Laurence drew to write. She always said *A Bird in the House* was her most autobiographical work of fiction and denied that her other books sprang from her life, but as she said in 1963: "One's writing is not meant to be bound up with one's life, but only jerks believe this."[15] She claimed *The Stone Angel*'s characters weren't her, "naturally, although some of them are, in some ways, as must surely always be the case,"[16] but then admitted she had many of Hagar's characteristics, especially in how she hated to feel beholden to anyone. She said Stacey of *The Fire-Dwellers* wasn't her, but then Stacey also drank, dieted, had an affair, and was riddled with the same guilt and fear about the world as Laurence felt then. Laurence also said Morag of *The Diviners* wasn't her, but "talks in one of my voices."[17] Then, as with Stacey, the similarities ran deeper. Morag was an orphan and a writer who sacrificed her marriage for writing, then anticipated the end of her career. She was also scared in big cities, reluctant to show her husband her first novel, and fought to leave Manawaka, only to find it was part of her and she had to make peace with those who raised her. Laurence finally concluded as she finished *The Fire-Dwellers* in 1968: "I don't write directly out of personal experience, but all the same I often wonder how much of myself I'm revealing in novels and stories—in fact, I'm revealing the whole thing, but I always fondly hope that this isn't obvious to everyone. And, in a peculiar way, the characters are definitely not me, while at the same time expressing aspects of myself."[18] Swayze told me: "Many times I heard her say, when asked when and where she taught school, that she had never been a spinster school teacher like Rachel Cameron, just as she had never been a ninety-year-old dying woman, but the experience of those fictional characters revealed some of the depths in her own experience."

That trend of mining her life for her fiction became even more obvious as she began to include others from her circle in her books. She told Wiseman that both she, Adele, and Jack, Laurence's ex, were in *The Diviners,* and while Morag's husband, Brooke, wasn't Jack, "some of the underneath emotional things are the same." She added: "[P]eople are going to call this novel highly autobiographical, and in some ways it is, altho the main character's background (is) pretty different from my own." But after struggling with the personal strains that were emerging in this book, she concluded: "I know I have to go on and write it the way it wants to be written, but it bothers me. The echoes reaching into one's own life, I mean. I don't seem to have done such a good camouflage job this time. They've all been there before, but better painted."[19]

One of the other advances Laurence made in this time was finally developing some of the writing community that she'd been seeking since she left college. It didn't come quickly. She'd gone to England hoping to find such a community, but despite some effort, she only met a few British writers and never developed a broader base there. She made a few friends, renewed a few acquaintances, and attended some CBC staff members' parties. She met Mordecai and Florence Richler after Jack McClelland asked them to introduce themselves. She also freelanced for awhile to keep from becoming a recluse, and joined the Canadian Universities Society, where she was the program director who arranged speakers for a year. But, by 1967, she wrote Purdy that despite trying not to be isolated, she was not succeeding. Still, her writing community was slowly growing. In the early 1960s, her initial contact was exchanging letters with such writers as Wiseman, Ethel Wilson, and Jane Rule. But the more Laurence's reputation grew, the more she met other writers in Canada. Her "tribe" expanded, with many Canadian writers—including the Purdys, Gary Geddes, and Margaret Atwood—visiting her in England. Some guests stayed for dinner; others remained for

weeks. Percy Janes, the Newfoundland writer who wrote
House of Hate, even boarded with her in England for several
months in 1971. In 1974, Atwood wrote: "Young Canadians
somehow made a beeline for her house, and because of her
love of people and conversation and the difficulty she has
saying no, she wound up running a cross between a hotel and
an Ann Landers bureau."[20]

Laurence was well-known for supporting young writers,
which followed the pattern Ethel Wilson and her Manitoba
mentors set, but she also became friends with many of them.
Myrna Kostash said Laurence encouraged her to marry her
boyfriend there, providing a bouquet of sweet peas from her
garden for the ceremony. Laurence then congratulated Kostash
on finding her voice when she published her first book, *All of
Baba's Children*. Geddes recalled how important it was when
she, a major writer, confirmed his feelings about his work. She
also gave him a reference for the Canada Council. Geddes, a
lapsed Baptist, said they also "talked about social justice and
the lack of social gospel in so many churches."[21] But, by 1972,
Laurence said it was time to go home: "I have about 3 friends
in this country. I have about three dozen in Can."[22]

What's less well-known is that Laurence also emotionally
supported many senior writers. She met Paul Hiebert, the
retired chemistry professor who wrote *Sarah Binks*, when she
was in Winnipeg to receive her honorary fellowship from
United College in 1966, and they enjoyed a long correspon-

dence in which she encouraged his writing. She met Sinclair Ross in Montreal in 1967 and told him how much *As For Me and My House* meant to her, then persuaded McClelland to publish Ross's *The Lamp at Noon and Other Stories* in 1968 and she wrote the introduction. A decade later, she was one of the writers who planned to ask the Canada Council for financial aid for Ross, but he refused the help. Hugh MacLennan attended her 1969 McGill appearance and they supported each other by letter for many years. It was a pattern that she continued in Canada.

Laurence began considering a move back to Canada more seriously after her 1967 trip there. As she wrote to Wiseman, she returned "filled with more affectionate feelings towards Canada than I have harboured in many a long year, so naturally began thinking 'Could I live here again?'" She was torn about the idea for awhile since she liked connecting with African writing in England, but she grew to love Canada again through her cottage and growing network of friends. She also realized that her income, publisher, and friends were all based there. So, when her son, David, graduated from high school in 1973, she sold Elm Cottage and its furnishings to a neighbour to save it from suburban development. He then rented it to her friends, the Camerons, who invited David to stay. When she left for Canada on July 22, 1973, she had her cottage and a year of writer-in-residencies to ease the transition and was anxious to see what her future brought next.

CHAPTER 23

SETTLING IN ONTARIO

Laurence planned to wait a few months to buy a home, but by August, she knew what she wanted—an old house within walking distance of the shops in Lakefield, Ontario. Lakefield was a small town located thirty-two kilometres from her cottage, and Laurence found exactly what she envisioned the first time she called a Lakefield realtor. It was a two-storey brick home with three bedrooms, a study, and a self-contained apartment she could rent to a Trent student. She decided it was even more perfect after the couple to whom she rented it while she was still writer-in-residence sheepishly told her that it was recently a funeral home. She later wrote: "My own grandfather, on my mother's side, had been an undertaker, and the funeral home came into all my Canadian fiction in one way or another. I thought it was very appropriate."[1] It was interesting that five years later she also told me, "I hope I'll live there until I die," which is exactly what happened.

When I met Laurence, I asked why she chose Ontario, and she said she had friends across Canada, but more there, and it was close to her publisher. She never mentioned that she remained fearful of returning to Neepawa, where she no longer had family, but which may have impacted any thoughts of returning to Manitoba. She'd also given up on the idea of moving to the "Vile Metropolis" of Toronto, a good thing since she wouldn't take subways and rode white-knuckled when friends chauffeured. Clara Thomas said Laurence sat in their living room with a compass and drew a hundred-mile radius around Toronto to see where to live, but the die was cast once she bought her cottage. Laurence liked Peterborough, had friends there, could bus to Toronto, and maintain some proximity to friends while preserving her privacy. Jean Cole of Peterborough also said that Laurence liked Lakefield for the same reason: "She liked to be one step removed."[2]

Laurence was a woman sensitive to place, which made me wonder if there was more to her choice. My husband and I drove to Peterborough one spring evening so I could meet her friends and learn more about the last decade of her life. We'd barely left the 401 to head north-east on 115 when I started staring at the silhouetted contours. The land was rolling; the trees bare along the highway. "This could be the TransCanada south of Neepawa," I kept repeating, peering into the gloom. "That's why she liked it here. It looks just like home." I could barely wait to start for Lakefield the next morning, but daylight only confirmed my conclusion. It was, except for the Otonabee River, the same geography where we both grew up and the only part of southern Ontario I'd seen that resembled it, but that made me wonder if there were also other connections.

I stopped at the Lakefield library, marvelling as I scanned the town. Here were the wide streets and core of prosperous stores that mimicked Neepawa. The post office stood apart, and the mix of blond and red brick buildings echoed her hometown. After my first appointment, I admired Laurence's portrait in the library, then asked the librarian how to find 8 Regent Street. "Margaret Laurence's house?" she asked, and I nodded. "Straight down Queen Street and turn right." Unsolicited, she added: "She was such a nice woman. She always smiled and said 'Hi.'"

The house was easy to find. A few folks tried to turn it into a writers' centre after Laurence died, but they later sold it. The family home across from St. James Anglican Church now had a memorial plaque on the front lawn. The house looked like its pictures from Laurence's time, except that there were now white wicker chairs on the front porch. I studied it, trying to see the resemblance to her grandfather's house that so many noted. Her Lakefield home was a boxy beige brick house of a similar vintage with a porch, but it didn't have a flight of stairs to the porch as did her grandfather's Neepawa house. What struck me most, however, as I looked around, was that it was situated exactly like her Neepawa home—near the end of the main street and a few houses off—and I remembered what Swayze had told me: "She created another Neepawa wherever she lived."

The prairie connections thickened at Trent University, three kilometres from her house. She received an honorary degree from Trent in 1972, served her last writer-in-residency there from January to May 1974, and was chancellor from 1981 to 1983. She liked its restored urban buildings and forested main campus that looked like Clear Lake, but it was its spirit that reminded her of United College. As she wrote in her memoir: "I grew to respect, admire, and love it as a small liberal arts and science university of the kind I had known when I myself was young."

Laurence enjoyed Trent's community from the start. The Mortons and local writer Jean Cole became friends after her 1969 speech. She liked the small classes where people got to know each other, so she returned to speak to Canadian studies and literature classes for years after working there. She also sat on its *Journal of Canadian Studies'* editorial board from the mid-'70s until just before she died. John Wadland, a Canadian Studies professor who was the journal's associate editor then, said Trent also had a number of professors either from or interested in the prairies, including Orm Mitchell, author W.O. Mitchell's son. Laurence usually attended the journal's editorial board's meetings and enjoyed the stimulating discussions about Canada's political and cultural landscape, where she could discuss everything from Quebec separatism to history and literature with such prominent Canadians as Morton, and Claude Ryan of Quebec.

Laurence appreciated Trent's founding philosophy with its social gospel approach of being involved in the community. "Margaret was the incarnation of the social gospel and she would have found a real home here for the social gospel," Wadland said, noting she felt "you cannot just talk, you have to give back."[3] She took that approach seriously as chancellor when she publicly challenged the new president, Donald Theall, whenever she felt he wasn't living up to Trent's standard. She also enjoyed giving honorary degrees to her heroes, Tommy Douglas and Malcolm Ross, and delivering the citation for Lois Wilson's degree. Jean Cole added that Trent was extremely supportive of Laurence, always including her in social gatherings and finding people willing to drive her. Like United, it offered both friendship and a progressive intellectual community, even though Swayze later said she rarely stayed longer than absolutely essential in public gatherings, while she could visit for hours with friends in private homes.

The first year back in Canada, Laurence took the two writer-in-residencies for money, but they helped her begin to build her place in the Canadian community. As she noted in September 1973: "I'm not all that broke right at the moment, but I think my Depression sense of insecurity is still very operative. Odd— on the one hand, I feel I have to stash $$$ away for my old age, and on the other hand I am convinced I won't live to see 60."[4]

While serving as writer-in-residence, she advised students, attended classes, gave readings, and even visited high schools, for, as she wrote Al Purdy, "my motto is Grab 'Em For the Cause Of Canwriting, Young!"[5] Laurence recalled being lonely while at London's University of Western Ontario in the fall of 1973 because her kids were in England, but John and Angela Graham said that she tended to keep to herself after hours when her school commitments were done. She still found a group of former Manitobans, including the Grahams, in its English department and even made enough community connection that she agreed to return to speak at the London Regional Art Gallery's luncheon program in 1985. She spent the Christmas of 1973 with friends and extended family, then found life a little easier at Trent, for she lived on campus and enjoyed having students drop in to visit. She also began to make the connections that proved so valuable for the rest of her life.

Laurence was never writer-in-residence again after Trent. She started rejecting requests the first fall in London and eventually turned down two in Manitoba. I was disappointed to learn that one of them was at the University of Manitoba in 1976–77 while I was still a student. My English professor, David Arnason, had arranged the invitation and Purdy, then its writer-in-residence, extended it. She even refused former classmate Bedford's invitation to go to United College, then the University of Winnipeg, in 1980. She said she needed to write, but she really found the demands on a writer-in-residence too exhausting. As she said in 1980: "I believe that a writer-in-residence should earn her or his salary, (and in this not all writers agree with me), but I know that my own tendency was ... to take on far too much and to become exhausted."[6]

Despite not having a formal position, Laurence continued to enjoy her connections with children and youth. She had several godchildren and many friends commented on how much their children liked her. Anne Graham in London, the Grahams's now-adult daughter, told me Laurence was "cool" and helped her assemble her dad's doodled drawings into a book and name it. Alice Olsen Williams, near Lakefield, said her children remembered Laurence's kindness and her daughter liked to visit Laurence after her skating lessons in Lakefield. A notice from Toronto's Children's Book Centre in Laurence's archived files said she frequently read and talked to local schools because she felt the children were hers. She also visited a range of high schools and universities. Teachers and professors told me that once her nervousness wore off, she thoroughly engaged the students. She even enjoyed answering their questions because she said she didn't feel she had to "perform" as for adults. It was a fascinating link that carried forward the legacy of her Neepawa, Winnipeg, and Vancouver mentors while also showing her sense of social responsibility for the next generation.

Laurence moved into her Lakefield home on May 1, 1974, and soon grew to love it as much as Elm Cottage. She spent her Trent term as writer-in-residence buying antique and second-hand furniture, and as with the cottage, loved purchasing the rest from Eaton's catalogue. She found her place in Lakefield and wrote another ex-Manitoban writer, Gabrielle Roy, in 1977: "I think I am beginning to feel like a villager, and to be accepted as such." People called her by name and she helped whenever asked. She was one of the judges for the Queen Victoria Look-Alike Contest at Lakefield's Victoria Days Celebration in 1981. Like her mum in Neepawa, she also supported the Lakefield Public Library, donating books and appealing to the town council to give it a new, accessible home. She also supported its fundraising, allowing the Lakefield Readers' Theatre to use an excerpt from *The Fire-Dwellers* for a fundraiser. She even vacated her house for a day soon after she was diagnosed with cancer because the library had sold a thousand tickets for people to take a tour of it. This was a new time and place in Laurence's life, but the prairie writer had come full circle back to live in a small Canadian town.

CHAPTER 24

THE WRITERS' TRIBE

Laurence was finally reconnecting with community, but she found one of her strongest links to be with other Canadian writers. Her major bond was with The Writers' Union of Canada, but she was also involved in launching its offspring, the Writers' Development Trust.

Laurence had been pro-labour since her Winnipeg days and was deeply interested in the Union that Toronto's writers began developing in the early 1970s. It emerged after the Ontario government established a Royal Commission on Book Publishing to look at the American takeover of Canadian publishing houses and didn't call for any writers' submissions. A number of writers spoke anyway, then a group—including Margaret Atwood, Graeme Gibson, and June Callwood—banded together to begin building connections. They organized a Toronto meeting of Canadian writers in December 1972 and a conference in June 1973, then asked Laurence to be the interim chair. She agreed and spent the fall of 1973 travelling from London, Ontario, to Toronto to draft a constitution with the interim executive. She considered accepting its invitation to be the first chairperson, too, but after wrenching her back and breaking a bone in her foot, she decided the stress of even contemplating that leadership role was too much, and she wrote Al Purdy: "It just ain't me, Al. I cannot do it. I'll go on a committee, but I will not be the front person."[1]

The Writers' Union formed in November 1973 and Laurence was involved for nine years. She regularly attended conferences and encouraged other writers to join because she believed the Union raised important questions about writers' rights and their status in society. She sat on its first membership committee and chaired its first Emergency Committee to help writers with grant applications, publisher hassles, or accommodation when visiting other cities. She worked on the committee reviewing fees, helped draft the Union's model trade book contract in 1976, and was involved in the late 1970s campaign to prohibit Canadian bookstores from importing remaindered foreign editions of Canadian books. She also encouraged the Union to review the writer-in-residence role and cautioned it not to take nationalist or political stands that imperilled members' relations with their publishers. Laurence even used her connections with the Canadian publishing industry to lobby for desired changes. When she was a member of McClelland and Stewart's board for three years, she tried to persuade it to adopt the Union's model contract. Former Trent professor Christl Verduyn said she also argued passionately that the *Journal of Canadian*

Studies' editorial board should acknowledge the work of those who made their living writing by signing contracts with them, recognizing their copyright, and compensating them. As Laurence later wrote: "It was a heady time for us, and indeed an extremely important time, for it brought together writers from all over Canada and gave us a sense of true community in this enormous land."[2]

Laurence gave the Writers' Union credibility and helped it define itself as a tribe. She'd used that term since living in Africa, and just before he died, prominent Canadian writer Pierre Berton proudly told me: "That was a wonderful phrase and we were a tribe." He called her "heroic" to be interim chair since she was so shy, but he added: "[I]t needed someone of her stature to be out in front because she had a public persona. She was the top writer then. She was the person who epitomized what we wanted to do.... She was the spirit of the Union in the early years." He said she believed writers needed a union because "we were worried about copyright, agents, and contracts."[3] Fellow writer Graeme Gibson, who helped found the Writers' Union, added that "she was a passionate believer who did all that she could. Her willingness to be the interim first chair of the union (against many of her own instincts, and despite her fears), and lending her name and presence to all sorts of strong causes, was extremely valuable and personally admirable."[4]

The Writers' Union established the Writers' Development

Trust in 1977 and Laurence, Gibson, and Berton were its first board members. The Union started the Trust to accept donations for it, but also hoped that the Trust would help develop Canadian literature and support writers in need. Gibson and the Union's executive director, Alma Lee, did most of the initial work, but Laurence attended its first meeting and stayed on the board until 1979. She remained an honorary patron into the 1980s, despite her concern about how the Trust was developing and whether she was personally liable for the debts from its unsuccessful fundraising dinners. She always promoted the educational resource booklets that several writers and teachers developed for the Writers' Union and the Trust then offered to schools so they could teach Canadian literature. When Laurence's publisher, Jack McClelland, became the Trust's chairperson, she also attended the fundraising dinners despite her dislike of being the attraction.

Following the pattern that she had established in England, Laurence also continued to support many writers. She corresponded with more than one hundred Canadian and British authors, and wrote Canada Council references for their grants, "tender messages" for their book covers, and numerous book reviews. She wrote to a range of friends and strangers, making perceptive comments about their work, encouraging people from B.C. short story writer Jack Hodgins to *Chatelaine* editor Doris Anderson, and maintaining a long correspondence with several senior writers. One was Ernest Buckler in Nova Scotia, whose book of short stories she helped to have published. Another was Hubert Evans, the almost-blind B.C. writer who was in his eighties. He refuelled on her support and wrote three more poetry books and an autobiographical novel. She even visited him in his home when he was a frail ninety-two and read his citation as "the elder of the tribe" when Simon Fraser University awarded him an honorary doctorate in 1984. As she wrote Wiseman immediately after: "It was one of the most moving days of my entire life."[5]

Laurence's support for writers never ended, but her affiliation with the Writers' Union did. Wiseman and a few writers left the Union in 1979 when June Callwood became chair, as they were unhappy that it included non-fiction as well as fiction writers. Laurence and Wiseman had been friends for more than thirty years and many agreed that Wiseman was, as her friend Sylvia Fraser said, "like a terrier" while Laurence always remained a little deferential to her. But the two were like family, so when Wiseman left the Writers' Union, she encouraged Laurence to go, too.

Laurence struggled with that decision for three years. She wrote Wiseman in February 1980: "I *do* share some of your concerns, while not able to share all of them."[6] But then she began to withdraw from the Union. Laurence never attended another annual meeting and started writing letters to the Union expressing her concerns. She feared it would make the model contract more complicated, and suggested that it reduce the organization's size to live within its fees and not rely on government funds. She also opposed any suggestion its membership directory be seen as a reference book of Canadian prose writers since it excluded forty major writers. The Union rebutted her concerns, but she resigned on October 8, 1982, saying she didn't "feel bound to remain in an organization whose ideals and aims I can no longer endorse." She still felt the Union wasn't monitoring the Trust enough and was also so reliant on government support that it couldn't strongly protest the cruise missile tests. She was so concerned about the Writers' Union ignoring Canada Council guidelines and sending mediocre writers to readings that she also wrote Naim Kattan of the Canada Council about it in November 1982, a month after she resigned from the Union, and said she spent "three years of anguished deliberation" before resigning. Laurence's biographer, Powers, said Laurence joined Adele Wiseman's new social club that started meeting in 1982, but many of the people I talked to said she always wished she could rejoin the Union.

CHAPTER 25

MOUNTAINS AND VALLEYS

The 1970s were Laurence's personal peak, but also her deepest valley. She was celebrated by her hometown, then persecuted in the censorship debate. It was a period that forever altered her life, sending her back to the church but also ensuring that she never wrote adult fiction again.

By the mid-1970s, Laurence was a celebrity. She won the Molson Prize and a second Governor General's Award for *The Diviners* in 1975. She published her essay collection, *Heart of a Stranger,* in 1976, became a Fellow of the Royal Society in 1977, and chaired the Governor General's fiction committee in 1978. The National Film Board even made a documentary on her, *Margaret Laurence—The First Lady of Manawaka*, which premiered in Winnipeg. But the honour she appreciated most was having her hometown of Neepawa celebrate her on October 6, 1975.

The Neepawa and District Community Schools suggested that she be invited to attend a Margaret Laurence Day. Although some didn't like her books because of the "language," the idea caught on and she agreed. When the day arrived, she spent the morning talking to high-school students who were studying Canadian literature and gave them her usual pitch that it was their birthright to have such a literature. She also proclaimed the same message to forty English teachers at lunch and recommended the Writers' Union's resource booklets to them. Laurence then toured her old hometown and saw the cemetery where her parents were buried, her former homes, and the new library. By the time several Manitoba journalists interviewed her, she declared the town looked more prosperous than it had in 1949, then noted it had had a profound effect on her, though she never told them what that effect was. That evening, about 125 people, including her former teacher Mildred Musgrove and friends Laurence hadn't seen in thirty years, attended a dinner at the Legion Hall. The mayor made her an honorary citizen and gave her an engraved cornucopia representing Neepawa, plus architectural drawings of her grandfather's home. She was moved to tears during four standing ovations and said: "The visit to Neepawa means more to me than any other recognition I have ever had of my work because it comes from my own people. It is a memory which I will cherish all my life."[1]

It sounded wonderful, but many felt her distance. One former neighbour had volunteered to help with the dinner to meet her again, but didn't feel she could approach her. Another said Laurence often sat alone that night. I'd chalked it up to shyness until Wayne Boyce, a friend who was the *Brandon Sun* reporter that day, told me that he found her reticent to talk about Neepawa: "She refused to say anything and wouldn't be pushed. It was like I got a sudden glimpse of a troubled soul with memories and associations that if she spoke freely about, she would not make friends for herself." He felt she was vulnerable and couldn't don a mask: "Once we got on to other questions, she was fine, even kind, but in a tired way." That picture left me wondering if she really had processed her past to the degree she claimed when writing her Manawaka fiction.

Four months after Laurence returned to Lakefield, she was hit by the censorship scandal. In early 1976, two parents objected to *The Diviners* being taught to Lakefield's Grade 13 students. The principal withdrew the novel until the school board's Textbook Review Committee could review it, even though it was on the Ministry of Education's approved list and he'd already read it and agreed that his English Department head, Bob Buchanan, could teach it. Buchanan told me that he was ready for a challenge since the school board had surprised teachers by banning three books the previous year. He figured that they couldn't lose since *The Diviners* was a great book that deserved to be taught, Laurence lived down the street from the school and had been to his class, and she and the students liked each other. But, looking back, he wished he'd warned Laurence about the potential controversy before it began.

The storm of protest was larger than he expected. Stories and letters filled the local press for three months. Fundamentalist Christians lined up on one side behind school trustee Jim Telford, who wanted only Christians to choose school books. The Writers' Union and author Robertson Davies lined up on the other with local students, citizens, English teachers, and the Rev. Jack Patterson of Lakefield United Church to defend the book. Laurence initially spoke out, saying the language and sex scenes were necessary to the story, then maintained a "dignified silence" until it was over. She was shocked by the attack, but didn't feel that she should have to defend her work. She was also shaken to the core because she believed that she'd written a "profoundly religious" book but was being called a blasphemous pornographer by people too naive to see the morality in her work. The Textbook Review Committee—a mix of trustees and public—unanimously approved *The Diviners* and the school board voted ten to six to allow it, but the local Pentecostals continued their assault until the school board reaffirmed its decision. Renaissance Peterborough, a conservative group based out of Trent, then tried but failed to get more fundamentalist trustees elected that fall.

Everyone who knew Laurence commented on how that attack devastated her. Buchanan felt she was so badly wounded that it weakened her, and Bill Whitehead believed it was the reason she never wrote again. During the ordeal,

Laurence drew friendship and strength from such people as Joan Johnston, a local citizen who helped to organize the fight to support *The Diviners*. When the initial battle was done, Laurence told the *Peterborough Examiner:* "I wasn't out to ruin the moral fibre of the nation." She later said in her memoir: "It had felt like a gift of grace to me to be able to write it. I was shocked and hurt by this hostility." What finally troubled her most was that the attacks came primarily from fundamentalists: "With my sense of being a Christian, or at least an aspiring Christian with an ecumenical outlook, I felt extraordinarily damaged."

Laurence regrouped, but was never the same again. She researched the topics of censorship and pornography and gave a speech to Ontario's provincial judges in 1983, then wrote an article for *Toronto Life* in 1984. She even lent Alice Munro her notes to counter her book-banning attacks. Ultimately Laurence's issue became one of free speech. As she later said, she opposed pornography, but "I worry that censorship of any kind might lead to the suppression of anyone who speaks out against anything in our society, the suppression of artists, and the eventual clamping down on ideas, human perceptions, questionings."[2]

Laurence's research helped her marshal her arguments for the second censorship attack in December 1984. This time a local municipal councillor with two children in Lakefield Secondary School tried to rally support to have the school board remove *The Diviners, A Jest of God, The Stone Angel,* and J.D. Salinger's *Catcher in the Rye* from the curriculum. The councillor's municipal council initially supported her, then withdrew its support when her campaign failed to gain much momentum. This time Laurence decided to fight. She was angry and stronger, and even though it drained her, she spent months doing local and national interviews, denouncing the move to ban these books as an attack on current Canadian writing. That April, the school board's Textbook Review Committee unanimously vindicated all four books and the board voted overwhelming to let its classes use them. The councillor threatened to go to court to enforce her wishes, but nothing came of it, and the censorship forces again failed to muster more electoral support.

Laurence won both fights, but always remained troubled about her attackers. One of the things that bothered her most was that they called themselves Christian, but their views were antithetical to hers. She later wrote: "I realize that the people who are convinced they have the only answers, and who feel they have the right to impose their wishes and views on everyone else, will probably always be with us, and we must remain on guard." But she also believed that those who tried to ban her books were individuals who "don't believe in sex education for young people, who are always anti-abortion under any circumstances, and who yet maintain they believe in Christian love. It seems to me that what they're in fact preaching is hatred, authoritarianism, and a suppression of humankind's thoughts, queries, and aspirations."[3]

Laurence countered some of this destruction by returning to the United Church in 1977. She later said that she quit attending the Unitarian church because of its hymns: "[A]lthough I agreed with many of their concepts of faith and their very progressive outlooks, I couldn't stand the hymns, which I call 'spirit of Light' hymns, very abstract and boring."[4] While she'd long struggled with the Christian concepts of virgin birth, Jesus's divinity, and personal immortality, she'd always prayed, read her Bible, and believed that a Holy Spirit informed both creation and her writing. She appreciated Lakefield's Anglican and United Church support in the 1976 censorship debate, and Lois Wilson wrote that Laurence also "grasped the central affirmation of Christian faith, the Incarnation—that God in all tenderness became one of us and dwells with us, but she had had difficulty appreciating the institutional expression of that belief."[5] Laurence told an interviewer during this period: "I would say I have always been a fairly religious person in a fairly unorthodox way."[6] But Swayze said she discovered that her convictions were really Christian, and despite the faults of formal Christianity, she wanted to be part of a worship community.

During the late 1970s and early 1980s, Laurence talked a lot about the importance of including the "female principle" in the Holy Spirit. She wrote Nigerian writer Chinua Achebe in 1984 that she had that belief confirmed while reading about Ghana's indigenous faiths, especially the Akan, so she changed hymn words to feel included. As she noted: "I disagree deeply with many of the concepts in some of the old hymns of the Protestant churches (Onward, Christian Soldiers, for example ... terrible), but they are in some ways noble hymns and I suppose are also so deeply a part of my childhood and my heritage, so I love them and frequently change some of the words when I go to church." Her friend Doris Dyke, then a professor at the United Church's Emmanuel College in Toronto, said Laurence struggled with the male-dominated religion of her past, but often addressed God as "Sir or Madam." She also wrote prayers in inclusive language, which were widely used. She even supported Almuth Lutkenhaus's *Crucified Woman* sculpture when it was condemned by some of the same fundamentalists who attacked her books. The sculpture, now behind Emmanuel College, portrays a woman hung in the form of a cross. Laurence later wrote: "To me, she represents the anguish of the ages, the repression, the injustice, the pain that has been inflicted upon women, both physically and emotionally. 'Crucified Woman' also speaks to me of the comfort and help I have known from my mothers and the unconditional love I feel for my own children.... 'Crucified Woman' is almost dancing, on the earth, the life dance of pain and love."[7]

Laurence's distress deepened through these years as she tried to write another novel and failed. While she had long prophesied that *The Diviners* would be her last book, she later noted: "I didn't know how much it would hurt."[8] She'd written since she was a child, couldn't imagine doing anything else, and once said that "the only thing worse than writing is not writing."[9] She kept trying until at least 1983, but didn't want to do a "mock-up" of a novel and Clara Thomas told me that Laurence could never get the voices right. Laurence wrote in 1986: "[I]t has finally become clear to me that the novel I thought I wanted to write was simply not there to be written."[10]

Laurence's spiritual and prairie roots were obvious in the topics she tried to explore for that novel. She attempted to write on the fundamentalists, but told Bob Buchanan: "I eventually realized that I was writing this book to get even, that I was abusing my gift."[11] Swayze said she told writer Robert Kroetsch that she'd been given a novel on the Selkirk Settlers, but when Swayze drove her through Winnipeg's North End in 1978, she wanted to visit the Ukrainian Labour Temple and other reminders of her North End and *Citizen* experience. She wrote Wiseman in 1979 that she'd begun to "question whether I *really* want to write *fictionally* about the Old Left in Winnipeg."[12] Biographer Powers found drafts of a novel called *Dance on the Earth* with a Ukrainian and a Scots-English family, but Laurence wrote Wiseman in 1981 that she had learned that "I cannot ever write about another cultural and ethnic background from the inside." I saw the beginning of a *Dance on the Earth* novel in her papers at York.

It had two women dancing as they closed a cottage for the season, and she'd scrawled across the top: "July 1983 I am not going to write this novel." These were difficult years and she constantly ended letters with "I am not in despair," but finally admitted to Hubert Evans and Gabrielle Roy that she was despairing.

What was working, though, were three children's books. They all drew on her sense of place, but also touched on her responsibility, ancestry, and spiritual themes. She published the first two books in 1979. Former Manitoban James Lorimer issued *Six Darn Cows* as part of his young children's series. It was the simple tale of two children on a farm, similar to one located near her cottage, who learned to take a risk in order to be responsible. Laurence was excited about writing another song for it, and Lorimer recorded it for the book's promotion. She also wrote *The Olden Days Coat*, which first appeared in *Weekend Magazine* before she expanded it for McClelland and Stewart. This was the charming tale of Sal, ten, who discovered a magical coat in her Gram's trunk and travelled back to meet her Gram as a child. Laurence said that she wrote the story after she visited a doctor north of Lakefield who had an antique sleigh collection. She was delighted when he invited her to take a ride since she hadn't been in a cutter since she was a child. The book drew on her themes of past and present, and some illustrations were also included of her Lakefield home and neighbourhood.

Laurence's last book, *The Christmas Birthday Story*, was published in 1980 and reflected her spiritual roots. She'd written her version of the nativity story for her children's Unitarian class in Vancouver in 1959 after another parent wanted to abolish the Christmas pageant because everyone knew angels couldn't fly. Laurence later explained why she had written the story. "I was very upset and said I would not want my own young children to be deprived of that most important part of their heritage."[13] She lost the manuscript when she moved to England, but met a woman at a Lakefield dinner party who sent her a copy that she had kept since her Unitarian days in Vancouver. Laurence considered it a gift, so published it, and was always proud of the story that emphasized her beliefs that the nativity was about the birth of a beloved child in a loving family and Jesus "grew up to be a wise teacher, and a friend to all people." She also incorporated a twist that reflected her views on gender—that Mary and Joseph didn't mind whether the baby was a boy or girl, as long as it was healthy.[14] That change angered some fundamentalists, since Luke 1:30–31 says that the angel told Mary she'd have a boy. Laurence's story also contained another quirk that reflected her past. She used her African experience to describe how fast the kings' camels ran, ringing the silver bells on their leather reins and saddles.

Laurence had some playful moments during these years, but her worries often outweighed her pleasures. She and Clara

Thomas compiled a cookbook. They cited the first Canadian cookbook in Catharine Parr Traill's *Canadian Settler's Guide* as their inspiration, and lightheartedly noted that their cookbook was for people like themselves who would rather talk than cook. But Laurence's health issues became a growing concern. She was diagnosed with diabetes in 1974, and within a decade, she had arthritis in her right hand, carpal tunnel syndrome in her right wrist, and was almost blind in her right eye until she had surgery. She had growing financial worries, though her generosity continued and she kept running up huge phone bills as part of her lifeline to friends. When she asked Hugh MacLennan and Alice Munro to provide references for a major Canada Council grant in 1980, both agreed, but MacLennan suggested that she also ask the university of her choice for a part-time job because any English department would snap her up and she could earn a basic living. She refused, insisting that she had to write. But, as she wrote Purdy that year, she was becoming more angry that "the work of writers such as you and myself and quite a pile of others, have become a kind of growth industry in the academic world, and here we are, damn it, wondering every January if we're going to make enough to live on this year."[15]

Friends also believed that her drinking escalated after the 1976 censorship debate, and many commented on how she'd make late-night calls, sometimes playing bagpipe music, and alienating many people whom she'd known. Long-time colleagues stopped visiting because they found her morose and repetitive. She also always seemed lonely, and she would cry about the state of the world and talk about her failed marriage. Several friends felt that she always loved Jack—she often commented "God, he was handsome!"—but, at York, I came across a copy of a note that she sent to Timothy Findley in 1981 that said she admired his partnership with Bill Whitehead because she had never found a "relationship of equals." As she once said, she'd known one man well and a few others peripherally, but none of them could ever form that kind of relationship with her.

Some of Laurence's friends were afraid to intervene with her drinking, and those who did paid a steep price. Budge Wilson said Laurence's Lakefield friends didn't try to talk to her about it because they knew she would resent them. Some writing friends, however, decided to take action. Biographer King said Atwood talked to Laurence's daughter, Jocelyn, about their concerns and word got back to Laurence through Wiseman. Laurence was furious that Atwood had not only interfered, but had called her daughter. She was also angry with Marian Engel and Timothy Findley for defending Atwood. She shunned Atwood, but made up with Engel and Findley, emotionally supporting Engel when she battled cancer in 1983. No one I met ever tried another intervention.

CHAPTER 26

CITIZENSHIP: A SOCIAL RESPONSIBILITY

People often have currents that run in and out of their lives like tides. By 1980, Laurence's fiction was done and she was starting to engage in the activism that had been one of her life's undercurrents. The peace movement became her main focus, but she also addressed prairie and national issues, and some women's concerns. Working on such causes gave her a way to turn her social gospel sense of responsibility from words into action, but it also gave her the opportunity to exercise her celebrity power and strong convictions to make a difference in the world.

Despite her long absence from the west, Laurence always defined herself as being a prairie person. She moved to Lakefield twenty-five years after leaving Manitoba, but wrote in 1976: "I am basically a prairie writer, even though I have written of other places. My emotional attachment to the prairies remains very strong."[1] She still loved the crunchy snow, vast farmlands, and black soil that "seemed the only proper colour for soil to be,"[2] but her attachment wasn't just sentimental for she also encouraged a new generation of prairie writers. She spoke at a literary conference at the University of Saskatchewan in 1977 and supported the *NeWest Review*, which began in Edmonton in the 1970s, by subscribing to it, writing a book review of a new writer's work, and buying thirty-six subscriptions for friends. George Melnyk, its editor then, told me that connection provided her with a sense of the dynamic west, but she was also a "godmother whose encouragement was needed and valued."[3]

Even when speaking on national issues, Laurence often did it from a prairie perspective. Alma Lee, the Writers' Union's former executive director, said, "she was a national writer who was very conscious of the regional conscience."[4] When a group of writers decided to form a Toronto Union chapter in 1979, she spoke against it as a prairie writer from outside Toronto, decrying the impact it would have on the Union. When Gary Geddes edited *Divided We Stand,* a book he hoped would reach out to Quebec during its 1977 sovereignty crisis, she contributed "Listen. Just Listen." It spoke of her trip to Louis Riel's grave and Batoche, when she was in Saskatchewan in 1977, and how she'd heard the voice of all of their ancestors on the wind. She appealed to those in Quebec to remain part of the nation and encouraged them to listen to other Canadians who also wanted to shape a new country for everyone. She even signed "Canada & Quebec: A Proposal for a New Constitution," which appeared in the *Canadian Forum.*

Laurence supported the New Democratic Party (NDP) and women's activism. She joined the NDP and wrote a 1980 fundraising letter for the national party to encourage people to support Ed Broadbent. Lynn McDonald, who briefly served on the Energy Probe board with Laurence, recruited her to be the star attraction at her fundraising dinner when she ran as an NDP candidate for a federal seat in Toronto. Laurence then served on the board of McDonald's charitable trust, the Three Guineas Foundation, which allocated McDonald's money to support women's, peace, and environmental projects. As an honorary director of the Canadian Abortion Rights Action League (CARAL), Laurence also publicly defended a woman's right to a legal abortion by signing CARAL's first successful fundraising letter in 1982. She also gave a reading to help York University's Women's Centre in 1983, and it passed some of the funds to CARAL.

Laurence's major commitment in her last years, however, was the peace movement. The nuclear spectre had haunted the world for forty years, but there was a growing concern in the 1980s about the potential role of nuclear proliferation in a global confrontation, and she lent her passion to trying to stop a nuclear war. In the spring of 1986, she said: "I feel more and more that not only am I a writer, but a citizen of this country and of the world and I feel very, very strongly compelled ... to take a much more active part in the peace movement as a social activist of one kind and another. Those viewpoints have been consistent throughout my years, but I'm much more active than I once was."[5] She had joined ten peace organizations by 1982, but within a year scaled back to four, though she kept responding to the fifty letters she received a week.

Laurence's peace work covered a broad range. She was a member of the interfaith disarmament group Project Ploughshares, and mostly worked with it nationally. She wrote protest letters to the government and a foreword to the book *Canada and the Nuclear Arms Race*, then contributed to its signed newspaper ads and spoke at its Mother's Day Walk for Peace in Peterborough in 1983. She also supported Operation Dismantle, which held municipal referendums to try to stop the U.S. from testing its cruise missile in Canada. She promoted Operation Dismantle in various speeches and signed its 1986 open letter to Prime Minister Brian Mulroney protesting nuclear warship visits to Canada. She was briefly honorary chairperson for Arts for Peace in 1982, and spoke at its conferences and rallies until she discovered that the group wasn't formally organized, so she left it. She was also affiliated with The Group of 78, some prominent Canadians who held a 1984 conference on Canadian foreign policy and concluded that the United Nations needed to be strengthened to build a just international order and achieve peace and security. Her work was so prominent that the National Film Board even produced a second short film, *A Writer in the Nuclear Age: A Conversation with Margaret Laurence*. It was released a year before she died and showed how deeply she was moved about peace issues, including the nuclear threat, writers' social responsibility, and the power of ordinary people to influence events.

Laurence was a passionate member of Energy Probe's board from 1982 to 1986. As with Trent's journal, she loved the lively discussions, but she also wrote its two most successful fundraising letters protesting nuclear proliferation and Ontario Hydro's use of tritium, which could refresh nuclear weapons. She wrote Prime Minister Trudeau opposing the sale of CANDU reactors to repressive regimes, and Members of Parliament to alert them to the tritium issue, then exchanged pointed letters with Ontario Hydro, finally obtaining a joint meeting with its officials.

Laurence often spoke at everything from rallies to convocations during these years, but her message was usually the same. She called peace the most pressing issue of the time, noted politicians' folly in believing that they could survive a nuclear attack, and called on Canada to help achieve world disarmament. She talked about the need to protect the world's children and how the 550 billion dollars spent on world armaments could improve the human condition. She often referred to the social gospel and said her faith made her believe something could be done to stop the arms race. She also routinely called on others to speak out and join the movement. When she addressed the youth, she displayed the same passion that she had as a high-school newspaper editor during World War II. She encouraged them to become citizens who non-violently protested cruelties, social injustice, civil liberty infringements, and government indifference, and her message often brought thunderous applause. As she told York University students in 1980: "We must continue to proclaim those things we believe in—the possibility of true communication between human individuals and between people of all cultures; the responsibility of those of us in lands rich in food and natural resources to help people in lands suffering from famine and deprivation; the sheer *necessity* ... of peoples to live in peaceful co-existence with one another and with the other creatures that share our planet, and our responsibility to protect and restore the earth itself."[6]

CHAPTER 27

CROSSING OVER

By the time Laurence turned sixty on July 18, 1986, she'd finished the first draft of a memoir she started in the 1970s, but was worried about her brother Bob in Alberta, who'd just been diagnosed with cancer. Her friend Joan Johnston threw a party for her on July 19, using the money that York University's archives paid for her files on the censorship fight, and Laurence's friends took great delight in toasting the fundamentalists who made her celebration possible.

The party at Johnston's, just outside of Lakefield by the Otonabee River, was a success—friends whom she called after noted that she sounded happier and more confident than she had in years—but Laurence was so short of breath that she frequently sat in the gazebo. Johnston attributed it to the humidity, but a month later, Laurence's breathing was so bad that she ended up in hospital. This time the diagnosis was terminal lung and kidney cancer, the same as her brother's, with only six months to live. Laurence cancelled a writer's tour overseas and started worrying about how she'd finish her memoir. Johnston brought in the tape recorder she'd given Laurence to tape the African highlife records that she was wearing out. Laurence dictated and Johnston typed. By the time they finished the second draft in November, Laurence was too sick to continue. She passed the manuscript to her daughter, Jocelyn, to prepare *Dance on the Earth* for publication.

Laurence's brother died that fall and Laurence became weaker. Johnston helped with her laundry and errands until Laurence's tenant moved out and her son, David, and his wife, Sona, moved into the suite in her house. Laurence filled seven journals that Johnston gave her as she talked to God and made peace with her life. As she wrote Wiseman, it was helpful to write what was happening, but: "This 'passage' (my situation now) is a humbling experience, like writing."[1]

Then, in early December, Laurence fell on some ice outside the suite and broke her leg, and many said that's when she gave up. She'd raised her kids and written her books, and felt that her life was finished. What she most feared was dying the way her mum had and putting her children through that. On January 4, 1987, she had a long talk with Johnston, who'd been her most frequent companion since Johnston retired a few years earlier. Johnston said Laurence spoke of crushing pills and drinking the powder, but Johnston thought it was too soon to discuss that. Even though Laurence knew the cancer wasn't spreading as quickly as initially expected, she didn't want to wait too long in case she couldn't take the final step on her own. She also refused any suggestion that her friend help since she knew the law and didn't want Johnston implicated.

David and Sona were away on January 5, so Johnston arranged for Bell to install a portable phone to help Laurence, now stuck in a hip-to-toe cast and living on the main floor. The door was unlocked. So when Laurence's friend Alice Olsen Williams, who'd earlier arranged to take her a quilted wall-hanging that day, called and didn't get an answer, she phoned Johnston and they agreed that Williams would check in since Johnston was doing her post-Christmas cleanup.

"It was a beautifully sunny day," Williams recalled, sitting by her dining room window overlooking Curve Lake, north of Lakefield, as we talked. She remembered finishing her TV show that day, then taking the shortcut across the lake. "I drove across the ice and said to myself, 'What am I going to do if she's dead?'" When she got to Laurence's, she found Bell's calling card. "I opened the door real quiet. She might have been sound asleep, she was having trouble sleeping. I took my boots off. She had a hospital bed in the living room, and there were curtains there. She was in bed and I went over. I didn't know. I was scared, but I didn't want to touch anything, so I went outside and went to her neighbour's."

The neighbour to the south, whom Laurence had often talked about, wasn't home, so Williams went to the other neighbour's and asked to use the phone to call police. She was so shaken that she couldn't find the number in the book, and when the neighbour asked why, Williams said: "I think my friend next door has died." Remembering, Williams continued on. "She came right over and knew. She called the police, then I called Joan." The police, doctor, and ambulance soon arrived, immediately followed by Johnston.

Williams studied the lake as she finished her story. She waited a long moment, then turned to me, her eyes meeting mine. "I felt she was here with me for a long time afterwards."

I nodded. I knew exactly what she meant. There had been times since I started this project that I, too, had sensed Laurence's very strong presence, as commanding in death as it was in life.

CHAPTER 28

ALL ROADS LEAD HOME

A year after my first research trip to Neepawa, I stood by Laurence's grave at Neepawa's Riverside Cemetery. She was buried there in June 1987 when her children visited to open the Margaret Laurence Home. Johnston told me that an autopsy had shown that Laurence wasn't dying of cancer, but asbestosis. I knew that both her mum and brother had died young from similar cancers, so I wondered if there was asbestos in one of her Neepawa homes, which were all still occupied.

I'd stopped by the Margaret Laurence Home before driving to the cemetery. The volunteers I'd met a year earlier were still struggling financially to keep it going. They'd had a Margaret Laurence reading corner in the Manawaka Gallery for four years before the Neepawa Area Development Corporation gave them $10,000 toward saving the house from demolition. The fall before she died, Laurence learned that the Margaret Laurence Home Committee was buying her grandfather's home. Walter Swayze said that he was surprised she agreed because she had angrily rejected most other honours at the time. But she wrote the committee in November 1986: "I was delighted to learn that the old Simpson house has been purchased. It means a very great deal to me that the old brick house will remain in the town and will survive." She specifically asked that it be a living centre, not a museum, but she didn't live long enough to see it officially opened on June 24, 1987. That was left to her children, who arrived the day before to bury her ashes. They'd never been to Neepawa before, but had been raised on her pictures and stories. Jocelyn told the crowd at the ceremony: "Our family history had always been central to our idea of who we are ... and Neepawa was one of the touchstones of that identity."[1]

The Margaret Laurence Home now is Canada's only physical memorial to Laurence, but other tributes have proliferated since her death. The Writers' Union set up an annual memorial lecture. So did Trent, which already had a scholarship in her name to help Canadian literature and Canadian studies students. Laurence's children gave her library to Trent's Catharine Parr Traill College, where it is still intact in a meeting room. The University of Winnipeg established the Margaret Laurence Collection of Literary Texts and the Margaret Laurence Chair to encourage an activist link to the community. Energy Probe set up the Margaret Laurence Fund to foster an understanding of peace and the environment. The Lakefield Literary Festival was started on the July weekend closest to her birthday, and the Lakefield United Church hosts the festival's guest speaker. Laurence's books were translated into several languages and studied by international scholars. I'd wondered if they were still being taught in schools when I met an English professor from Israel and a nursing professor from York University who both taught them, and Swayze said that a professor from Japan had recently visited him. There had been symposiums and stamps honouring her, and many women told me Laurence was still their favourite author. I wondered how she, a private woman, would have liked all of that. But Rabbi Arthur Bielfeld, who became her friend when he chaired Energy Probe's board, said, "[I]t keeps her memory alive."[2]

I walked around Laurence's grave. It had a grey granite headstone carved simply with her name, dates, and a Celtic cross. It matched the simple exterior of the woman I had met thirty years earlier, and I think she would have liked its location, overlooking the river in the ravine and the green hilly golf course across from it. Both of her parents, her paternal grandfather, and an infant uncle were buried nearby in the Wemyss plot, mere feet from where Neepawa's first homesteaders had built their home. The town historian had shown me the remaining corner of that first home's foundation, and it seemed appropriate to have such a historic marker from Neepawa's beginning resting so close to the woman who spent her life dealing with her past and ancestry.

I stood overlooking the grave and valley. Now we were both back in the place we began, only this time it was my turn to have gained a new perspective from studying Laurence's life and work. The first lesson I learned was the importance mentors played in her life as she developed her writing career. Her mother and teachers encouraged her as a teen, providing her with honest criticism that improved her work and her view of what she could do. That left me wondering how many people had that kind of support for their life's passion, and how many provided that to others. What could we become with that affirmation? And what could we do to better launch our teens?

I also learned the price of following one's spiritual call, the price that Laurence paid to live her life's purpose. I'd long since left journalism to write fiction, girded by her belief that it was hard to do both simultaneously. But studying her life, I realized the price she'd paid to live her life's purpose was the price I must pay to finish my novel. It took her more than a decade to write a novel that she could publish. Having worked as long on mine, I found it heartening that someone of her later stature struggled so hard to launch her career; it added incentive to keep going against what felt like insurmountable odds. I also discovered that the price she paid to do her best fiction was what I'd been reluctant to pay for mine because I knew where it would lead—right back to my prairie and family roots, the very place she didn't want to go, either, when she started her Manawaka fiction. But, if what I most admired about her work was its raw honesty, then I needed that, too.

She also showed me the importance of shouldering the obligations of one's calling. For, like Laurence, I'd been raised to believe writers were marginal and their work was a hobby to be done after the real work was completed. Now I'd seen the power of literature to speak the truth across time and space, and I knew there was nothing inconsequential about that.

I'd also seen an arc to Laurence's life, which tied all of her values and life choices back to her prairie roots. There was a remarkable consistency that fed not only her writing and sense of social responsibility, but her concept of place, community, and spirituality. It was all fostered before she left Neepawa, and then honed in Winnipeg. Its fruit blossomed as she claimed her place in the world. That left me wondering how many lives would play out with the kind of consistency that hers had, tying so many themes from the beginning to the end. She stayed the course, despite all of her disappointments along the way, and our lives were enriched by her gift.

I'd also learned from her sense of social responsibility—the message she tried to pass to her inheritors. The economics for writers, one of Canada's key cultural producers, hadn't changed much in the sixty years since she launched her career. They remained much like the economics for farmers, the primary producers in another key Canadian industry. It was discouraging, but no more than the other social injustices she flagged. Some of the nuclear threat had abated, but little else had changed. If anything, there was more need for community, a local grounding of people to face the erosion that globalization had caused in the intervening years. At least now writers had some community in the Writers' Union, much as farmers had in their co-operatives and wheat pools. There was a reason these began, and a reason they still existed. That banding together to address people's concerns was what Laurence felt the social gospel called us to do, especially for the good of those who don't have even our advantage to fight for improvements. It was time to accept our collective social responsibility to make the world a better place. Laurence couldn't say it often enough in her last years, but I couldn't help wondering how many had really listened.

I've heard the story many times now. A crowd of Laurence's friends and supporters, and several dignitaries, was at the Margaret Laurence Home when it was officially opened in June 1987. A huge storm had been brewing for hours, and funnel clouds were passing on the horizon. The crowd wondered if the ceremony should be held on the front lawn, but there were too many people to move inside, so the speeches proceeded. Ivan Traill, one of my relatives who chaired the Margaret Laurence Home Committee then, had arranged to have white pigeons symbolizing doves fly from the Home. It was symbolic because, in southwestern Manitoba, a bird in the house means a death in the family. Laurence knew that when she had a sparrow in "A Bird in the House" fly into Vanessa's room just before Vanessa's dad died in the same way as Laurence's dad had died. Laurence was now gone, too, and the pigeons represented not only her peace work, but the Holy Spirit that infused her writing, and a death finally being freed from the Home. The birds were placed between the front and storm windows, the latter being the old-fashioned kind with three round air holes in the bottom, the type that Laurence described in her story. As the words of the official opening were spoken, the storm window was opened and the pigeons were released. They flew up and over the tree tops into a brilliant sky and a double rainbow in the east. Many of those who were there said that the double rainbow felt like a blessing on all that had occurred.

Margaret Laurence struggled in life, but she was a great writer because she mined her soul to answer her spirit's call. She drew from a sense of place, community, spirituality, and social justice that was formed on the prairies, and made a significant imprint on the world. She has been gone for twenty years, but many of us, her inheritors, are still being graced by her spirit. I like to think that the double rainbow on the day the Margaret Laurence Home opened was also the Spirit's blessing for those of us left to follow her lead and answer our calls to better serve the world.

ACKNOWLEDGMENTS

Writing this book has been a wonderful journey, and I'd like
to thank those who helped:

- Althea Prince and Susan Silva-Wayne, my editors, for
  signing the project and allowing it to grow to fruition,
  Martha Keenan, for bringing her production skills to
  the project, and Kim Echlin, for leading me to
  Canadian Scholars' Press/Women's Press;

- Walter Swayze, who so lovingly read the manuscript
  and provided his insightful comments to ensure that
  it was both accurate and informed, and Margaret
  Swayze for her insights;

- Jocelyn and David Laurence for their permission to
  access, and include, Margaret Laurence's material,
  and Susan Drinkwater for her permission to access,
  and include, Jack McClelland's;

- the Ontario Arts Council for its Writers' Reserve grants;

- Joan Johnston, and Clara and Morley Thomas for
  their guiding wisdom and assistance;

- the many Neepawa people who were so willing to help—Pat and Ivan Traill, Dorothy Campbell Henderson, Betty Chisholm and Joyce Kingdon of the Margaret Laurence Home, Cecil Pittman, Dorothy Brown, Howard Alguire, Allan Drysdale, Jeanette Sutherland, and Dean Dietrich;
- Gerald Bedford, Hedda Ben-Bassat, Pierre Berton, Arthur Bielfeld, Wayne Boyce, Jock Brown, Bob Buchanan, Jenny Carter, Jean Cole, Doris Dyke, Sylvia Fraser, Rosemary Ganley, Gary Geddes, Graeme Gibson, John, Angela, and Anne Graham, Julia Harrison, Marian Hebb, Myrna Kostash, Louise Kubik, Alma Lee, John Lennox, Gail Lindsay, Ian Manson, John Martyn, Lynn McDonald, George Melnyk, Mona Meredith, Mary Mindess, Bill Metcalfe, Helen Porter, Judy Pinto, Janis Rapoport, Laurence Solomon, Christl Verduyn, John Wadland, Ron Ward, William Whitehead, Alice Olsen Williams, Budge Wilson, and Lois Wilson for sharing their material and memories;
- Lascelle Wingate and the staff at The Writers' Trust of Canada; Deborah Windsor and the staff at The Writers' Union of Canada; Suzanne Dubeau, Sean Smith, Michael Moir, and the staff at York University's Clara Thomas Archives; Carl Spadoni of The William Ready Division of Archives and Research

Collections at McMaster University; Ann Goddard of
Library and Archives Canada, and the staff at Trent
University's archives, University of Winnipeg's
archives, and Manitoba Legislative Library.

ENDNOTES

CHAPTER 2. GROWING UP PRAIRIE

1. Bill Whitehead, interview by author, Toronto, September 2004.
2. David Arnason and Dennis Cooley, "Outcasting: A Conversation with Margaret Laurence about the World of Manawaka," *Border Crossings*, 32.
3. Margaret Laurence, *Dance on the Earth* (Toronto: McClelland & Stewart, Inc., 1989), 53.
4. Michel Fabre, "From *The Stone Angel* to *The Diviners*: An Interview with Margaret Laurence," in *A Place To Stand On*, ed. George Woodcock (Edmonton: NeWest Press, 1983), 201.
5. Rosemary Sullivan, "An Interview with Margaret Laurence," in Woodcock, *A Place To Stand On*, 69.
6. Laurence, *Dance on the Earth*, 11–12.
7. Donnalu Wigmore, "Margaret Laurence: The Woman Behind the Writing," *Chatelaine*, February 1971, p. 54.
8. Paul G. Socken, ed., *Intimate Strangers: The Letters of Margaret Laurence & Gabrielle Roy* (Winnipeg: University of Manitoba Press, 2004), 35.

CHAPTER 3. THE ROAD TO THE BIG HOUSE

1. Laurence, *Dance on the Earth*, 24.
2. Laurence, *Dance on the Earth*, 55.
3. Laurence, *Dance on the Earth*, 63.

Chapter 4. A Writer's Sensibilities

1. John Parr, ed., *Speaking of Winnipeg* (Winnipeg: Queenston House, 1974), 68–69.
2. Margaret Laurence, "It Came Upon a Midnight Clear," in *Heart of a Stranger* (Toronto: McClelland and Stewart-Bantam Limited, 1980), 214.

Chapter 5. The Mask of the Bear

1. Laurence, *Dance on the Earth*, 40.
2. Laurence, *Dance on the Earth*, 61.
3. Laurence, *Dance on the Earth*, 69.
4. Laurence, *Dance on the Earth*, 64.
5. Laurence, *Dance on the Earth*, 74.
6. "Margaret Laurence's faith, hope and love," *The Whig-Standard*, October 15, 1979, p. 5.
7. Arnason and Cooley, "Outcasting," 33.
8. Laurence, *Dance on the Earth*, 76.
9. Margaret Laurence, letter to Lorna Nelson, May 4, 1983, The Margaret Laurence Home archives, Neepawa.

Chapter 6. High-School Journalism

1. Laurence, *Dance on the Earth*, 72–73.
2. Laurence, *Dance on the Earth*, 83.
3. Peggy Wemyss, "Editorials," *Annals of the Black and Gold*, Graduation 1944.

Chapter 7. Graduation: An Era Ends

1. Parr, *Speaking of Winnipeg*, 70.
2. Laurence, *Dance on the Earth*, 88.
3. Laurence, *Dance on the Earth*, 90.

Chapter 8. Winnipeg's United College

1. Parr, *Speaking of Winnipeg*, 72.
2. Clara Thomas, *Margaret Laurence* (Toronto: McClelland and Stewart Limited, 1969), 7.
3. Peggy Wemyss, Letter to the Editor, *Annals of the Black and Gold*, Neepawa, December 1944.
4. Margaret Laurence, letter to Lorna Nelson, May 4, 1983, The Margaret Laurence Home archives, Neepawa.

5. James King, *The Life of Margaret Laurence* (Toronto: Vintage Canada, 1997), 54.
6. Laurence, *Dance on the Earth*, 91.

CHAPTER 9. WAR LAYS A FOUNDATION

1. Margaret Wemyss, letter to Helen Warkentin, July 26, 1945, Margaret Laurence Collection, Clara Thomas Archives, York University, Toronto.
2. Margaret Wemyss, letter to Helen Warkentin, August 18, 1945, Margaret Laurence Collection, Clara Thomas Archives, York University, Toronto.
3. Laurence, *Dance on the Earth*, 98.
4. Laurence, *Dance on the Earth*, 100.
5. Laurence, *Dance on the Earth*, 99.

CHAPTER 10. MARRYING JACK LAURENCE

1. Laurence, *Dance on the Earth*, 93.
2. King, *The Life of Margaret Laurence*, 57.
3. Laurence, *Dance on the Earth*, 102.
4. Laurence, *Dance on the Earth*, 103.

CHAPTER 11. WINNIPEG'S NORTH END

1. Laurence, *Dance on the Earth*, 101.
2. Margaret Laurence, speech on opening the Bethune House at York University, Toronto, March 3, 1983, from the Margaret Laurence Collection, Clara Thomas Archives, York University.
3. Margaret Laurence, "North Main Car—Winnipeg," *Prairie Fire: Winnipeg in Fiction* 20, no. 2 (summer 1999): 100, 103.

CHAPTER 12. A NEWSPAPER CAREER

1. Laurence, *Dance on the Earth*, 107.
2. Parr, *Speaking of Winnipeg*, 73.
3. Margaret Laurence, interview by author, Winnipeg, October 1978.
4. Bill Ross, interview by author, Winnipeg, August 1980.
5. Bill Metcalfe, interview by author, Winnipeg, February 1978.
6. Margaret Laurence, interview by author, Winnipeg, October 1978.

CHAPTER 13. GLOBE-TROTTING

1. King, *The Life of Margaret Laurence*, 71.

2. John Lennox and Ruth Panofsky, eds., *Selected Letters of Margaret Laurence and Adele Wiseman* (Toronto: University of Toronto Press, 1997), 36.
3. Lennox and Panofsky, *Selected Letters*, 35.
4. Parr, *Speaking of Winnipeg*, 77.
5. Laurence, *Dance on the Earth*, 284.
6. Margaret Laurence, *The Prophet's Camel Bell* (Toronto: McClelland and Stewart Limited, 1963), 16.
7. Laurence, *The Prophet's Camel Bell*, 16–17.
8. Laurence, *The Prophet's Camel Bell*, 14.
9. Laurence, *The Prophet's Camel Bell*, 206–207.
10. Rosemary Sullivan, "An Interview with Margaret Laurence," in Woodcock, *A Place To Stand On*, 63.
11. Margaret Laurence, "The Very Best Intentions," in *Heart of a Stranger*, 25.
12. Laurence, *Dance on the Earth*, 153.
13. Sullivan, "An Interview with Margaret Laurence," 64.
14. Sullivan, "An Interview with Margaret Laurence," 63.

Chapter 14. Writing in Africa

1. Lennox and Panofsky, *Selected Letters*, 55.
2. Laurence, *The Prophet's Camel Bell*, 225.
3. Lennox and Panofsky, *Selected Letters*, 54.
4. Lennox and Panofsky, *Selected Letters*, 66.
5. Lennox and Panofsky, *Selected Letters*, 62.
6. Walter Swayze, interview by author, Winnipeg, October 2003.
7. Laurence, *Dance on the Earth*, 152.

Chapter 15. Life in Vancouver

1. Laurence, *Dance on the Earth*, 112.
2. Laurence, *Dance on the Earth*, 113.
3. Laurence, *Dance on the Earth*, 117.
4. Lennox and Panofsky, *Selected Letters*, 102.
5. Laurence, *Dance on the Earth*, 120.
6. Laurence, *Dance on the Earth*, 128.
7. Lennox and Panofsky, *Selected Letters*, 122.
8. Laurence, *Dance on the Earth*, 157.
9. Lennox and Panofsky, *Selected Letters*, 119.
10. Margaret Laurence, "Ten Years' Sentences," in *The Canadian Novel in the Twentieth Century*, ed. George Woodcock (Toronto: McClelland and Stewart, 1975), 235.

11. Alan Twigg, "Grappling with Reality," *NeWest Review* (December 1979): 4.
12. David Stouck, *Ethel Wilson: A Critical Biography* (Toronto: University of Toronto Press, 2003), 247.
13. Margaret Laurence, "A friend's tribute to Ethel Wilson," *Toronto Star*, January 24, 1981.
14. Twigg, "Grappling with Reality," 4.

CHAPTER 16. WRITING FROM AFRICA TO CANADA

1. Lyall Powers, *Alien Heart: The Life and Work of Margaret Laurence* (Winnipeg: University of Manitoba Press, 2003), 155.
2. Margaret Laurence, "Gadgetry or Growing: Form and Voice in the Novel," in Woodcock, *A Place to Stand On*, 82.
3. George Woodcock, "Jungle and Prairie," in Woodcock, *A Place to Stand On*, 230.
4. Sullivan, "An Interview with Margaret Laurence," 67.
5. Thomas, *Margaret Laurence*, 15.
6. Lennox and Panofsky, *Selected Letters*, 129.
7. Lennox and Panofsky, *Selected Letters*, 135.
8. Laurence, *Dance on the Earth*, 156.
9. Arnason and Cooley, "Outcasting," 33.
10. Lennox and Panofsky, *Selected Letters*, 135.
11. Lennox and Panofsky, *Selected Letters*, 136.
12. Lennox and Panofsky, *Selected Letters*, 142–143.
13. Laurence, *Dance on the Earth*, 157.
14. Laurence, *The Prophet's Camel Bell*, 1.
15. Laurence, *Dance on the Earth*, 157.
16. Lennox and Panofsky, *Selected Letters*, 142.
17. John Lennox, ed., *Margaret Laurence—Al Purdy: A Friendship in Letters* (Toronto: McClelland & Stewart Inc., 1992), 154.
18. Margaret Laurence, letter to Gordon Elliott, August 17, c. 1963, from Margaret Laurence Collection, The William Ready Division of Archives and Research Collections, McMaster University, Hamilton.
19. Laurence, "Ten Years' Sentences," 236.
20. Laurence, "A Place to Stand On," 15.
21. Laurence, "A Place to Stand On," 16.

CHAPTER 17. LIFE AT THE CROSSROADS

1. Laurence, *The Prophet's Camel Bell*, 47.
2. Laurence, *The Prophet's Camel Bell*, 53.

3. Laurence, *Dance on the Earth*, 149.
4. Sam Solecki, ed., *Imagining Canadian Literature: The Selected Letters of Jack McClelland* (Toronto: Key Porter Books Limited, 1998), 81.
5. Lennox and Panofsky, *Selected Letters*, 143.
6. Laurence, *The Prophet's Camel Bell*, 102–103.
7. King, *The Life of Margaret Laurence*, 117.
8. Lennox and Panofsky, *Selected Letters*, 103.
9. Lennox and Panofsky, *Selected Letters*, 154.
10. Laurence, *Dance on the Earth*, 158.
11. Lennox and Panofsky, *Selected Letters*, 144.
12. Laurence, *Dance on the Earth*, 157–158.

Chapter 18. Settling in England

1. Laurence, *Dance on the Earth*, 158.
2. Margaret Laurence, letter to Gordon Elliott, June 25, 1962, from Margaret Laurence Collection, The William Ready Division of Archives and Research Collections, McMaster University, Hamilton.
3. Laurence, *Dance on the Earth*, 158.
4. Laurence, *Dance on the Earth*, 159.
5. Lennox and Panofsky, *Selected Letters*, 151.
6. Lennox and Panofsky, *Selected Letters*, 154.
7. Lennox and Panofsky, *Selected Letters*, 156.
8. Lennox and Panofsky, *Selected Letters*, 155.
9. Lennox and Panofsky, *Selected Letters*, 278.
10. Laurence, *Dance on the Earth*, 166.
11. Laurence, *Dance on the Earth*, 169–170.
12. Donald Cameron, *Conversations with Canadian Novelists* (Toronto: Macmillan, 1973), 101–102.
13. Lennox and Panofsky, *Selected Letters*, 301.
14. Lennox and Panofsky, *Selected Letters*, 214.
15. Lennox and Panofsky, *Selected Letters*, 202.

Chapter 19. The Gift of Grace

1. Lennox and Panofsky, *Selected Letters*, 191.
2. Laurence, *Dance on the Earth*, 176.
3. Lennox and Panofsky, *Selected Letters*, 199.
4. Lennox, *Margaret Laurence—Al Purdy: A Friendship in Letters*, 108.
5. Parr, *Speaking of Winnipeg*, 79.
6. Margaret Laurence, "Jericho's Brick Battlements," in *A Bird in the House* (Toronto: McClelland and Stewart-Bantam Limited, 1978), 179.

7. Lyall Powers, "Margaret Laurence's Long Journey Home," in Centre for Great Plains Studies, *Great Plains Quarterly* 19, no. 3 (summer 1999): 206.

8. Laurence, *Dance on the Earth*, 185.

9. Michel Fabre, "From *The Stone Angel* to *The Diviners*," in Woodcock, *A Place To Stand On*, 203.

10. Laurence, "Ten Years' Sentences," 237.

11. Lennox and Panofsky, *Selected Letters*, 228.

12. Lennox and Panofsky, *Selected Letters*, 192.

13. Lennox and Panofsky, *Selected Letters*, 192.

14. Lennox and Panofsky, *Selected Letters*, 193.

15. Lennox and Panofsky, *Selected Letters*, 228.

16. Lennox, *Margaret Laurence—Al Purdy: A Friendship in Letters*, 57.

17. Lennox, *Margaret Laurence—Al Purdy: A Friendship in Letters*, 76.

18. Laurence, "Ten Years' Sentences," 240.

19. Lennox and Panofsky, *Selected Letters*, 301.

20. Wigmore, "Margaret Laurence," 52.

21. Laurence, "Ten Years' Sentences," 241.

CHAPTER 20. CHECKING OUT CANADA

1. Laurence, *Dance on the Earth*, 190.

2. Lennox, *Margaret Laurence—Al Purdy: A Friendship in Letters*, 174.

3. Lennox, *Margaret Laurence—Al Purdy: A Friendship in Letters*, 154.

4. Margaret Laurence, "W.L. Morton: A personal tribute by Margaret Laurence," *Trent Fortnightly*, Trent University, c 1981, p. 3, in Margaret Laurence Collection, Clara Thomas Archives, York University, Toronto.

5. Laurence, *Dance on the Earth*, 209.

6. Socken, *Intimate Strangers*, 89.

CHAPTER 21. *THE DIVINERS*

1. Laurence, *Dance on the Earth*, 198.

2. Lennox, *Margaret Laurence—Al Purdy: A Friendship in Letters*, 220.

3. Laurence, *Dance on the Earth*, 199.

4. Arnason and Cooley, "Outcasting," 34.

5. King, *The Life of Margaret Laurence*, 313.

6. Margaret Laurence, "Time and the Narrative Voice," in Woodcock, *A Place to Stand On*, 156.

7. Laurence, "Time and the Narrative Voice," 155.

8. Arnason and Cooley, "Outcasting," 34.

9. Laurence, "Ten Years' Sentences," 239.

10. Margaret Laurence, "A Place to Stand On," in Woodcock, *A Place to Stand On*, 18.

11. Laurence, "A Place to Stand On," 18.

12. Laurence, "A Place to Stand On," 17.

13. Laurence, "A Place to Stand On," 15.

14. Sullivan, "An Interview with Margaret Laurence," 70.

15. Sullivan, "An Interview with Margaret Laurence," 69.

16. Clara Thomas, "The Chariot of Ossian: Myth and Manitoba in The Diviners," *Journal of Canadian Studies* 13, no. 3 (fall 1978): 63.

17. Laurence, "Ten Years' Sentences," 238.

18. Lennox, *Margaret Laurence—Al Purdy: A Friendship in Letters*, 317.

CHAPTER 22. ROOTS AND WINGS

1. Laurence, "Ten Years' Sentences," 236.

2. Laurence, "A Place to Stand On," 19.

3. Laurence, "A Place to Stand On," 16.

4. Parr, *Speaking of Winnipeg*, 70.

5. Fabre, "From *The Stone Angel* to *The Diviners*," 198.

6. Margaret Laurence, letter to Gordon Elliott, November 25, 1962, in the Margaret Laurence Collection, The William Ready Division of Archives and Research Collections, McMaster University, Hamilton.

7. Lennox, *Margaret Laurence—Al Purdy: A Friendship in Letters*, 139.

8. Fabre, "From *The Stone Angel* to *The Diviners*," 194.

9. Clara Thomas, "Pilgrim's Progress: Margaret Laurence and Hagar Shipley," in Woodcock, *A Place To Stand On*, 162.

10. Laurence, "Ten Years' Sentences," 237.

11. "Why pick on Margaret Laurence?" *United Church Observer*, February 1980, p. 11.

12. Janice Acoose, *Iskwewak* (Toronto: Women's Press, 1995), 66.

13. Margaret Atwood, "Face to Face," in Woodcock, *A Place To Stand On*, 24.

14. Atwood, "Face to Face," 23.

15. Margaret Laurence, letter to Gordon Elliott, April 29, 1963, in the Margaret Laurence Collection, The William Ready Division of Archives and Research Collections, McMaster University, Hamilton.

16. Lennox and Panofsky, *Selected Letters*, 154.

17. Lennox and Panofsky, *Selected Letters*, 319.

18. Lennox, *Margaret Laurence—Al Purdy: A Friendship in Letters*, 82.

19. Lennox and Panofsky, *Selected Letters*, 319.

20. Atwood, "Face to Face," 21.

21. Gary Geddes, interview by author, Toronto, March 2005.
22. Lennox, *Margaret Laurence—Al Purdy: A Friendship in Letters*, 255.

CHAPTER 23. SETTLING IN ONTARIO

1. Laurence, *Dance on the Earth*, 210.
2. Jean Cole, interview by author, Peterborough, April 2005.
3. John Wadland, interview by author, Peterborough, April 2005.
4. Lennox, *Margaret Laurence—Al Purdy: A Friendship in Letters*, 286.
5. Lennox, *Margaret Laurence—Al Purdy: A Friendship in Letters*, 300.
6. Socken, *Intimate Strangers*, 81.

CHAPTER 24. THE WRITERS' TRIBE

1. Lennox, *Margaret Laurence—Al Purdy: A Friendship in Letters*, 296.
2. Laurence, *Dance on the Earth*, 207.
3. Pierre Berton, interview by author, Kleinburg, September 2004.
4. Graeme Gibson, e-mail to Noelle Boughton, Toronto, April 2005.
5. Lennox and Panofsky, *Selected Letters*, 389.
6. Lennox and Panofsky, *Selected Letters*, 355.

CHAPTER 25. MOUNTAINS AND VALLEYS

1. Undated and unattributed clippings, The Margaret Laurence Home archives, Neepawa.
2. Laurence, *Dance on the Earth*, 267.
3. Laurence, *Dance on the Earth*, 216.
4. Margaret Laurence, letter to Chinua Achebe, June 3, 1984, Margaret Laurence Collection, McMaster University Library Archives, Hamilton.
5. Lois Wilson, *Turning the World Upside Down* (Toronto: Doubleday Canada Limited, 1989), 232.
6. Fabre, "From *The Stone Angel* to *The Diviners*," 197.
7. Laurence, *Dance on the Earth*, 16–17.
8. Laurence, *Dance on the Earth*, 7.
9. Laurence, "Ten Years' Sentences," 235–236.
10. Laurence, *Dance on the Earth*, 6–7.
11. Bob Buchanan, interview by author, Buckhorn, April 2005.
12. Lennox and Panofsky, *Selected Letters*, 353.
13. Socken, *Intimate Strangers*, 58.
14. Laurence, *Dance on the Earth*, 221.
15. Lennox, *Margaret Laurence—Al Purdy: A Friendship in Letters*, 372.

Chapter 26. Citizenship: A Social Responsibility

1. Socken, *Intimate Strangers*, 17.
2. Socken, *Intimate Strangers*, 17.
3. George Melnyk, interview by author, Calgary, April 2005.
4. Alma Lee, interview by author, Toronto, March 2005.
5. Arnason and Cooley, "Outcasting," 34.
6. Margaret Laurence, "Open Letter to the Inheritors," York University convocation address, June 1980, in Margaret Laurence Collection, Clara Thomas Archives, York University, Toronto.

Chapter 27. Crossing Over

1. Lennox and Panofsky, *Selected Letters*, 407.

Chapter 28. All Roads Lead Home

1. Jocelyn Laurence's speech for the opening of the Margaret Laurence Home, June 24, 1987, The Margaret Laurence Home archives, Neepawa.
2. Arthur Bielfeld, interview by author, Toronto, Ontario, April 2005.

SELECTED BIBLIOGRAPHY

Acoose, Janice. *Iskwewak*. Toronto: Women's Press, 1995.

Arnason, David, and Dennis Cooley. "Outcasting: A Conversation with Margaret Laurence about the World of Manawaka." *Border Crossings* 5, no. 4 (November 1986).

Cameron, Donald. *Conversations with Canadian Novelists*. Toronto: Macmillan, 1973.

Centre for Great Plains Studies. *Great Plains Quarterly* 19, no. 3 (summer 1999). University of Nebraska-Lincoln.

Gunnars, Kristjana, ed. *Crossing the River: Essays in Honour of Margaret Laurence*. Winnipeg: Turnstone Press, 1988.

Heritage. *Neepawa Land of Plenty: 1883–1983: A History of the Town of Neepawa and District as told and recorded by its people*.

King, James. *The Life of Margaret Laurence*. Toronto: Vintage Canada, 1997.

Laurence, Margaret. *The Prophet's Camel Bell*. Toronto: McClelland and Stewart Limited, 1963.

———. *Long Drums and Cannons*. London: Macmillan and Co. Ltd., 1968.

———. *The Stone Angel*. Toronto: McClelland and Stewart Limited, 1968.

———. *Jason's Quest*. New York: Alfred A. Knopf, 1970.

———. *The Tomorrow-Tamer*. Toronto: McClelland and Stewart Limited, 1970.

———. *The Fire-Dwellers*. Toronto: McClelland & Stewart Limited, 1973.

———. *The Diviners*. Toronto: Bantam Books, 1975.

———. *A Jest of God*. Toronto: McClelland and Stewart-Bantam Limited, 1977.

———. *A Bird in the House*. Toronto: McClelland and Stewart-Bantam Limited, 1978.

———. *The Olden Days Coat*. Toronto: Tundra Books, McClelland & Stewart Young Readers, 1979.

———. *Six Darn Cows*. Toronto: James Lorimer & Company, Publishers, 1979.

———. *The Christmas Birthday Story*. Toronto: McClelland Stewart Limited, 1980.

———. *Heart of a Stranger*. Toronto: McClelland and Stewart-Bantam Limited, 1980.

———. "A friend's tribute to Ethel Wilson." *Toronto Star*, January 24, 1981.

———. *Dance on the Earth*. Toronto: McClelland & Stewart Inc., 1989.

———. *This Side Jordan*. Toronto: McClelland & Stewart Inc., 1989.

———. *A Tree for Poverty*. Toronto and Hamilton: ECW Press and McMaster University Library Press, 1993.

———. "North Main Car—Winnipeg." *Prairie Fire: Winnipeg in Fiction* 20, no. 2 (summer 1999).

Lennox, John, ed. *Margaret Laurence—Al Purdy: A Friendship in Letters*. Toronto: McClelland & Stewart Inc., 1992.

Lennox, John, and Ruth Panofsky, eds. *Selected Letters of Margaret Laurence and Adele Wiseman*. Toronto: University of Toronto Press, 1997.

"Margaret Laurence's faith, hope and love." *The Whig-Standard*, Kingston, Ontario, October 15, 1979.

Melnyk, George. "Margaret Laurence and the NeWest Review: An Appreciation." *NeWest Review* (March 1987).

Parr, John, ed. *Speaking of Winnipeg*. Winnipeg: Queenston House, 1974.

Powers, Lyall. *Alien Heart: The Life and Work of Margaret Laurence*. Winnipeg: University of Manitoba Press, 2003.

Socken, Paul G., ed. *Intimate Strangers: The Letters of Margaret Laurence & Gabrielle Roy*. Winnipeg: University of Manitoba Press, 2004.

Solecki, Sam, ed. *Imagining Canadian Literature: The Selected Letters of Jack McClelland*. Toronto: Key Porter Books Limited, 1998.

Stouck, David. *Ethel Wilson: A Critical Biography*. Toronto: University of Toronto Press, 2003.

Thomas, Clara. *Margaret Laurence*. Toronto: McClelland and Stewart Limited, 1969.

———. *The Manawaka World of Margaret Laurence*. Toronto: McClelland and Stewart Limited, 1976.

———. "The Chariot of Ossian: Myth and Manitoba in The Diviners." *Journal of Canadian Studies*. 13, no. 3 (fall 1978).

Twigg, Alan. "Grappling with Reality." *NeWest Review* (December 1979).

Wigmore, Donnalu. "Margaret Laurence: the woman behind the writing." *Chatelaine*, February 1971.

Wilson, Lois. *Turning the World Upside Down*. Toronto: Doubleday Canada Limited, 1989.

Woodcock, George, ed. *The Canadian Novel in the Twentieth Century.* Toronto: McClelland and Stewart, 1975.

———, ed. *A Place to Stand On: Essays by and about Margaret Laurence.* Edmonton: NeWest Press, 1983.

"Why pick on Margaret Laurence?" *The United Church Observer*, February 1980.

The Writers' Union of Canada. *Who's Who in The Writers' Union of Canada.* Toronto, 1993.